CW00422039

Que® Quick Reference Series

Microsoft Word® 5 Quick Reference

Bryan L. Pfaffenberger

Que Corporation
Carmel, Indiana

This book is based on Microsoft Word Version 5.0.

Que Quick Reference Series

The *Que Quick Reference Series* is a portable resource of essential microcomputer knowledge. Whether you are a new or experienced user, you can rely on the high-quality information contained in these convenient guides.

Drawing on the experience of many of Que's best-selling authors, the *Que Quick Reference Series* helps you easily access important program information.

Now it's easy to look up often-used commands and functions for 1-2-3, dBASE IV, WordPerfect 5, Microsoft Word 5, and MS-DOS, as well as programming information for C, Turbo Pascal, and QuickBASIC 4.

Use the *Que Quick Reference Series* as a compact alternative to confusing and complicated traditional documentation.

The *Que Quick Reference Series* also includes these titles:

1-2-3 Quick Reference
Assembly Language Quick Reference
AutoCAD Quick Reference
C Quick Reference
dBASE IV Quick Reference
DOS and BIOS Functions Quick Reference
Hard Disk Quick Reference
MS-DOS Quick Reference
QuickBASIC Quick Reference
Turbo Pascal Quick Reference
WordPerfect Quick Reference

Publishing Manager
Lloyd J. Short

Product Director
Karen A. Bluestein

Editor
Gregory Robertson

Technical Editor
Gregory Croy

Editorial Assistant
Fran Blauw

Indexer
Sharon Hilgenberg

Proofreaders
Lori Lyons
Peter Tocco

Table of Contents

Introduction 1

Hints for Using This Book 2

Accessing DOS 2

Adding Text 3

Aligning Text 3

Anchoring Text and Graphics 4

Annotating Text 6

ASCII Files 8

Automatic Styles 8

Autosave 11

Backing Up Your Work 12

Blank Lines 13

Boilerplates 14

Bookmarks 14

Borders and Boxes 16

Canceling Commands 17

Character Emphasis 17

Character Formats 18

Character Position 18

Choosing Commands 19

Clearing Documents 21

Clearing Word 21

Color 22

Columns 22

Command Area 23

Copying Formats 24

Copying Text 25

Cross-References 26

Cursor Movement and Scrolling 27

Customizing the Screen 29

Date and Time 30

Default Directory 31

Default Formats 32

Deleting Text 33

Division Breaks 34

Division Marks 36

Document Disk Full 36

Document Linking 37

Document Retrieval 38

Edit Command Menu 39

Fonts 40

Footnotes 42

Footnote Window 44

Form Letters 45

Forms 49

Function Keys 50

Glossaries 51

Graphics 54

Graphics Mode 55

Hanging Indentation 56

Headers and Footers 56

Headings 58

Help 59

Hidden Text 60

Hyphenating Words 61

Indenting Text 62

Indexing 64

Inserting Text 68

Joining Paragraphs 68

Jumping 69

Justifying Text 71

Key Status Indicator Codes 71

Learning Word 72

Line Breaks 72

Line Draw 72

Line Numbers 73

Line Spacing 75

Loading Documents 75

Macros 77

Mailing Labels 80

Margins 82

Math 83

Measurement Options 84

Moving Text 85

Newline Command.. 86

Numbering Series Items 87

Outlines 87

Overtype Mode 91

Page Breaks 91

Page Formats 92

Page Numbers 92

Page Size 94

Pagination.. 94

Paragraph Formats 94

Paragraph Marks 95

Previewing Your Document............................. 96

Previewing Page Breaks 98

Printer Selection 99

Printing 99

Quitting Word 101

Redlining 102

Replacing Formats 103

Replacing Text 104

Ruler Settings 105

Saving Your Work 106

Scrap 107

Scrolling with the Mouse 107

Searching for Formats 108

Searching for Text 109

Selecting Columns 110

Selecting Text 111

Show Layout 113

Side-by-Side Paragraphs 113

Snaking Columns 114

Sorting 115

Speed Key Shortcuts 116

Spell 117

Splitting Paragraphs 121

Spreadsheet Linking 122

Starting Word 123

Start-Up Options 124

Style Sheets 124

Summary Sheets 127

Tables of Contents 128

Tabs 130

Text Mode 133

Thesaurus 134

Transposing Text 135

Tutorial Help 135

Undo 136

Upper- and Lowercase 139

Windows 139

Index 144

Introduction

Microsoft Word 5 Quick Reference includes the quick
reference information you need as you create, edit,
format, and print Word documents, ranging from simple
memos to complex funding proposals and legal briefs.
Not a rehash of Microsoft's documentation, this book
includes the most frequently used information from
Que's best-selling publications on Microsoft Word 5.

Microsoft Word 5 Quick Reference is divided into
sections by tasks, applications, and topics. One section,
for instance, is called "Windows." Suppose that you are
in the midst of an editing session and you cannot
remember how to zoom a window to full size. Reach for
this quick reference guide—you will find the
information you want in the "Windows" section. Each
section of this book contains step-by-step instructions
for tasks Word 5 users undertake every day.

This book reviews Word 5 tasks, commands, and
procedures, but it is not meant to take the place of a
more comprehensive treatment of this extensive, flexible
program. It assumes you have already installed Word
successfully. This book does not attempt to teach you
Word concepts; it is for review and reference.

If you are new to Word, and especially if you're new to
personal computing, choose Que's *Using Microsoft
Word 5: IBM Version*, by Bryan Pfaffenberger. If you
have experience with previous versions of Word, or if
you are an intermediate to advanced user of other
software, you may prefer *Microsoft Word Tips, Tricks,
and Traps*, also by Bryan Pfaffenberger. After you read
these books, keep this quick reference guide next to your
computer—and when you need help remembering how
to carry out a task, reach for the step-by-step guidance
you will find in every page of this book.

Hints for Using This Book

As you read this book, keep the following conventions in mind:

> DEFAULT DIRECTORY. The title of a section in this quick reference guide. For more information, turn to this section.
>
> **T**ransfer **C**lear **W**indow. A Microsoft Word command name. To choose the command, type the boldfaced letters.
>
> font name. A field in a command menu. Press the **Tab** key to move to a particular field.
>
> **C:\MSWORD\LETTERS**. Characters you type.
>
> "Carry out the command" means to press **Enter** or click the command name.

This guide assumes you know how to choose Word commands and find your way through menus. If you need a quick review, see CHOOSING COMMANDS.

Accessing DOS

While working with Word, you can access DOS at any time by using the **L**ibrary **R**un command. Save your work before using **L**ibrary **R**un. Programs you run from DOS may not be crash-proof.

To access DOS

1. Save your work with **T**ransfer **S**ave (or **T**ransfer **A**llsave, if you have more than one document open or if you are using a glossary or style sheet) and choose the **L**ibrary **R**un command.

2. When the **L**ibrary **R**un command menu appears, accept Word's default command, and press **Enter**.

   Word displays the DOS prompt for the current DEFAULT DIRECTORY. You can use DOS just as you would outside of Word.

3. Perform the DOS operations you want.

4. At the DOS prompt, type **EXIT** to return to Word.

When you see the message `Press a key to return to Word`, press any key on the keyboard.

___

Caution

Do not use **L**ibrary **R**un to delete Word files while you are using Word; you may delete a file Word needs to complete the operating session, causing it to crash. To delete files, use the **T**ransfer **D**elete command. The **T**ransfer **D**elete command will not allow you to delete any necessary Word files.

Adding Text

By default, Word operates in insert mode. As you type, existing text moves forward and down automatically. You can work in the OVERTYPE MODE if you want. In the overtype mode, the characters you type erase existing text. To toggle between the insert and overtype mode, press **F5**. When Word is in the overtype mode, the code `OT` appears on the key status indicator. See also KEY STATUS INDICATOR CODES.

Aligning Text

With Word, text alignment—such as flush right, flush left, and centered—is a PARAGRAPH FORMAT. To change alignment, use the **F**ormat **P**aragraph command. You can choose alignments before or after you type.

___

To change paragraph alignment before you type

1. Choose the **F**ormat **P**aragraph command and select an option in the `alignment` field. Alternatively, press **Alt-R** for flush right, **Alt-C** for centered, or **Alt-J** for justified alignment.

2. Type the text. Every time you press **Enter**, Word repeats the alignment format automatically, so there is no need to issue the command again.

3. To return to the default paragraph format (flush left, single-spaced), press **Alt-P**.

___

To format paragraph alignment after you type

1. Place the cursor in the paragraph you want to format. Alternatively, select several paragraphs using a variable text selection technique (see SELECTING TEXT). To select the whole document, press **Shift-F10**.

2. Choose the **F**ormat **P**aragraph command and select an option in the `alignment` field. Alternatively, press **Alt-R** for flush right, **Alt-C** for centered, or **Alt-J** for justified alignment.

Anchoring Text and Graphics

Format p**O**sition is one of Version 5's most useful new features. With it, you can fix the position of a paragraph anywhere on the page so that it will remain there, even if you add more text above it.

"Paragraph" is used here according to Word's definition. The paragraph you anchor could be a paragraph of text, such as a sidebar that magazines use to emphasize a given passage. However, it could also be a graphic image imported with the **L**ibrary **L**ink **G**raphics command (see GRAPHICS).

An anchored paragraph is called a *frame:* a rectangular shape of fixed size and position. Once you have anchored the paragraph, the text you add to your document "floats" around the frame automatically. If there is room to the sides of the frame you have anchored, Word will automatically split the flow of text so that it flows past the frame to the left and right. You can place frames within multiple column text as well. When you use the **F**ormat p**O**sition command, you must specify how you want the frame anchored. To do so, specify a horizontal position and a vertical position. You may also control the amount of white space around the frame.

To anchor a frame

1. Place the cursor within the information about the graphic you want to position.

2. Choose the **F**ormat p**O**sition command.

3. In the `horizontal frame position` field, press **F1** to choose a horizontal alignment for the frame. You can also type a measurement.

   Choose from the following frame alignment options: **L**eft, **C**entered, **R**ight, **O**utside (on the outside of facing pages for two-sided documents), or **I**nside (inside of facing pages). The position can be determined relative to the edges of the page, the page margins, or the column margins.

4. In the `relative to` field, press **F1** to choose from the **P**age, **C**olumn, or **M**argins options.

5. In the `vertical frame position` field, press **F1** to choose from a list of alignment options. You can also type a measurement.

   You may choose from the following frame alignment options: **I**n line (not anchored vertically), **T**op, **C**entered, or **B**ottom. The position can be fixed relative to the top and bottom edges of the page or the top and bottom margins.

6. In the `relative to` field, choose from the top and bottom of the page or the top and bottom margins.

7. If you are positioning a graphic, press **F1** to choose the **W**idth of graphic option in the `frame width` field. Word will use the graphic width you chose with **L**ibrary **L**ink **G**raphic. If you are positioning a paragraph of text, however, type a measurement for the paragraph's frame width.

8. If you would like to add additional white space around the frame, type a measurement in the `distance from text` field.

   Word's default is 1/6th inch. You can increase this measurement if you want.

   Note: This measurement determines the distance from the text of all four sides of the frame, not just the top and bottom. If the frame is narrower than the text column, text will "float" around the frame to the left and right.

9. Carry out the command.

10. Check your work using Print preView.

Annotating Text

Annotations, a new feature of Word 5, makes Word more useful for collaborative writing. An annotation is like a FOOTNOTE, except its reference mark consists of up to 28 characters of text, and is not numbered by Word. Create an annotation using the Format Annotation command.

To add an annotation to your document

1. Place the cursor where you want the annotation's reference mark to appear.

2. Choose the Format Annotation command.

3. When the command menu appears, type your initials or your name in the `mark` field. You can type up to 28 characters.

4. Choose Yes in the `insert date` and `insert time` fields so that Word will insert the system date and time.

   If you are not using a clock/calendar board, you should set the system date and time correctly before starting Word. If you forget, press Esc to exit the Format Annotation command and use the Library Run command to run the built-in DOS programs called DATE and TIME.

5. Carry out the command.

   Word inserts the annotation number and the characters you have typed as the footnote reference mark; it echoes the number and text in the footnote area, and includes the date and time (if you selected these options).

6. Type your comments where Word has positioned the cursor (in the footnote area, after the end mark).

7. To return to the reference mark's location in the text, choose the **Jump Annotation** command.

To revise the text of an annotation

1. Select the reference mark of the annotation you want to edit.

2. Choose the **Jump Annotation** command.

   Word automatically scrolls to the annotation text of the annotation you have selected.

3. Revise the annotation as you would edit ordinary text.

4. Choose the **Jump Annotation** command to return to the annotation reference mark.

Do not try to delete an annotation by deleting all the annotation text in the annotation area. If you do, you will receive a `Not a valid action for footnotes or annotations` message.

To delete an annotation

1. Position the cursor on the reference mark.

2. Press the **Del** key.

Word cuts the annotation to the Scrap and removes the annotation text from the annotation area.

To move an annotation

1. Place the cursor on the reference mark and press the **Del** key.

   Word places the reference mark and the annotation text in the Scrap.

2. Move the cursor to the annotation's new location.

3. Press the **Ins** key or use the **Insert** command.

The FOOTNOTE WINDOW is a special window that automatically displays the text of the footnotes currently displayed in the document window. The footnote window displays annotations, too.

ASCII Files

Word users sometimes need to save their work as an ASCII text file, with hard carriage returns at the end of every line and no formatting codes. Such files are required, for instance, for most telecommunications applications.

To save your document as an ASCII text file, use the Transfer Save command and type a file name in the `filename` field. Then, choose the Text-only-with-line-breaks option in the `format` field.

Automatic Styles

You can change several important default formats using Word's automatic styles. An automatic style is a style that is applied automatically—that is, without the need to use the Format command or a speed key. These styles include:

- The character emphasis, font, and size used for page numbers inserted with the Format Division Page-numbers command. Normally, Word uses the default font for your printer. If you choose a special font for your document, the page numbers will not have this font unless you modify the automatic style.

- The position and format of the footnote reference marks inserted with the Format Footnote command. If you modify the automatic style, Word will superscript the reference marks automatically.

- The paragraph format of footnote text. If you modify the default format, you won't have to format each footnote individually.

- The default character font for your whole document. If you modify the default format, you won't lose special font formatting when you press Alt-space bar to cancel character emphasis.

You can save a great deal of time and frustration by creating automatic styles for these formats.

Previous versions of Word canceled the default SPEED KEY SHORTCUTS when you made changes to the default style sheet, NORMAL.STY. Word 5, however, does not cancel the speed keys. Most users will prefer, therefore, to make a few additions to NORMAL.STY rather than creating new style sheets. The instructions that follow assume you are modifying NORMAL.STY.

Note: When you start Word, it automatically loads the version of NORMAL.STY found in the DEFAULT DIRECTORY. You can place different versions of NORMAL.STY in each document directory you create. That way, when you start Word from a document directory, it automatically uses the version of NORMAL.STY appropriate to documents in that directory.

To change the default character format for page numbers

1. Choose the Gallery command.

2. Choose the Insert command. Leave the `key code` field blank. Choose Character in the `usage` field. Type **page number** in the `variant` field. Carry out the command.

3. Choose the Format command, and select a character format.

   If your printer handles multiple FONTS, choose a font name and font size you prefer.

4. Carry out the command, and use the Transfer Save command. Use the proposed response (NORMAL.STY).

5. Press Exit to leave Gallery.

To change the default footnote reference mark format

1. Choose the Gallery command.

2. Choose the Insert command. Leave the `key code` field blank. Choose Character in the `usage` field. Type **footnote reference** in the `variant` field. Carry out the command.

3. Choose the Format command, and select a character format.

Try choosing **S**uperscript in the `position` field and **Y**es in the `bold` field.

4. Carry out the command, and use the **T**ransfer **S**ave command. Use the proposed response (NORMAL.STY).

5. Press **E**xit to leave **G**allery.

To change the default format for footnote text

1. Choose the **G**allery command.

2. Choose the **I**nsert command. Leave the `key code` field blank. Choose **P**aragraph in the `usage` field. Type **footnote** in the `variant` field. Carry out the command.

3. Choose the **F**ormat **P**aragraph command, and select a paragraph format.

   Try choosing single line spacing, right-margin justification, and one blank line before.

4. Carry out the command, and use the **T**ransfer **S**ave command. Use the proposed response (NORMAL.STY).

5. Press **E**xit to leave **G**allery.

To change the default character font for your document

1. Choose the **G**allery command.

2. Choose the **I**nsert command. Leave the `key code` field blank. Choose **P**aragraph in the `usage` field. Type **standard** in the `variant` field. Carry out the command.

3. Choose the **F**ormat **C**haracter command, and select the font name and font size you want as the default.

4. Carry out the command.

   If you like, you now can redefine the standard paragraph format. Choose the **F**ormat **P**aragraph command, and choose the formats you want Word to use for all paragraphs (unless you override the default by giving a formatting command). You can choose justified alignment and an automatic first line indent.

5. Carry out the command, and use the Transfer Save command. Use the proposed response (NORMAL.STY).

6. Press Exit to leave Gallery.

Autosave

New to Word 5 is the autosave option in the Options command menu. This new feature automatically stores the changes you make to documents and, in the event of a power loss or computer failure, allows you to reconstruct work that you have not saved with the Transfer Save command. Its only drawback is that it consumes additional disk space. Therefore, if you are not using a dual floppy system or you are very short on disk space, you will want to use autosave all the time.

To turn on autosave

1. Choose the Options command and highlight the `autosave` field.

2. Type the number of minutes you want to elapse between backup operations. To back up your work every ten minutes, for instance, type **10**.

3. Carry out the command by pressing **Enter** or clicking on the command name.

To restore your work after a power failure

1. Restart your computer when the power is restored.

2. Start Word. You will see a message informing you that your work was not saved, and you are given the option of restoring these files.

Note: Using autosave is not the same as SAVING YOUR WORK. Even if you turn on autosave, you must still save your work to disk with the Transfer Save command.

Backing Up Your Work

To safeguard your work against disk failures or accidental erasures, make a backup copy of your work at the close of every operating session. New Version 5 features in the Library Document-retrieval command make it easy to back up your work by copying it to another disk.

To back up your work at the end of a session

1. Choose the Library Document-retrieval command.

   By default, Library Document-retrieval searches for all the .DOC files in the current DEFAULT DIRECTORY. To search for files in other directories, use the Query command.

2. When the list of files appears, highlight the first file you want to back up.

3. Press Enter to mark the file.

4. Choose the Copy option.

5. When the Library Document-retrieval Copy command menu appears, type the name of the destination drive or directory in the `marked files to drive/directory` field.

6. To copy the file to a backup file, choose the No option in the `delete file` field. To archive the file (remove it from your hard disk after it is copied to a floppy), choose the Yes option.

7. Carry out the command.

You can back up several files at once in a batch operation by marking them first. To mark a file, highlight it and press space bar or Enter. When a file is marked, an asterisk appears in the style bar to the left of the filename. To unmark a marked file, just press space bar or Enter again. To mark all the displayed files, press Ctrl-space bar. To unmark all of them, press Shift-Ctrl-space bar.

To back up several files in a batch operation

1. Choose the **L**ibrary **D**ocument-retrieval command.

2. Mark the files you want to copy by highlighting them and pressing **space bar** or **Enter**.

3. When you have finished marking all the files you want to back up, choose the **C**opy option.

4. When the **L**ibrary **D**ocument-retrieval **C**opy command menu appears, type the name of the destination drive or directory in the `marked files to drive/directory` field.

5. Carry out the command.

If you are backing up to a floppy disk and Word runs out of room on the disk, the copy operation will cease, and the files Word could not completely copy are left marked. Switch disks and choose the **C**opy option again to continue the operation.

Blank Lines

Avoid pressing **Enter** to create blank lines in your document. If you do, you will disable or limit several useful features, such as SORTING, and you will find it more difficult to prevent bad PAGE BREAKS. Enter blank lines with the **F**ormat **P**aragraph command or the SPEED KEY SHORTCUTS.

To enter a blank line before each paragraph as you type

1. Choose the **F**ormat **P**aragraph command and type **1** in the `space before` command field. Alternatively, use the **Alt-O** keyboard shortcut.

2. Type the text. Each time you press **Enter**, Word repeats the alignment format automatically, so there is no need to give the command again.

3. To return to the default paragraph format (flush left, single-spaced), press **Alt-P**.

To enter a blank line before a typed paragraph

1. Place the cursor in the paragraph you want to format. To select the whole document, press **Shift-F10**.

2. Choose the **F**ormat **P**aragraph command and type **1 li** in the `space before` command field. Alternatively, use the **Alt-O** keyboard shortcut.

Boilerplates

The term "boilerplate" refers to standard passages of text you use over and over again for a specific purpose. Attorneys maintain boilerplate files for standard contracts, such as wills. Businesses can use boilerplates for price lists or product descriptions. You can create boilerplates in two ways:

- Copy the boilerplate text to a glossary. You can retrieve the glossary's contents with a few keystrokes at any time (see GLOSSARIES).

- Create a Word document containing the text and insert it using the **L**ibrary **L**ink **D**ocument command (see DOCUMENT LINKING).

Of the two methods, the second is best for professional applications. It is easier to maintain a single, version of the boilerplate text by keeping it in a separate Word file.

Bookmarks

A new Word 5 feature called bookmarks greatly expands Word's boilerplating capabilities—and bookmarks have many other applications as well. A bookmark is simply a named unit of text, similar to a named range of cells in a spreadsheet. After you have named the range, you can refer to the range by its name, rather than typing the cell references. A bookmark is much the same. After you have named the unit of text, you can refer to it by name.

Once you have created bookmarks, you can use them in three ways:

- You can jump immediately to any bookmark in your document using the Jump bookmarK command (see JUMPING).

- You can cross-reference bookmarks so that, when Word prints your document, the program automatically fills in the correct page number on which the bookmark appears (see CROSS-REFERENCES).

- You can import bookmarks from other Word documents using the Library Link Document command (see DOCUMENT LINKING).

As you can see, bookmarks have more than one use, but a common one is to mark boilerplate passages for inclusion in other documents.

To mark text as a bookmark

1. Select the text you want to include in the bookmark.

   If you want the bookmark text to include its paragraph formatting, be sure to include the paragraph mark in the selection.

2. Choose the Format bookmarK command. When the command menu appears, type a name for the bookmark.

3. Carry out the command.

Every bookmark's name must be unique, and it must be one word. You can use up to 31 letters or numbers, and within the word you can use underscore characters, periods, and hyphens. Do not use colons, semicolons, or spaces. If you make a mistake, choose the Undo command immediately after using the Format bookmarK command.

To cancel a bookmark

1. Use the Jump bookmarK command to find and select the bookmark you want to cancel.

2. Choose Format bookmarK.

3. Leave the `name` field blank and carry out the command.

4. Press **Y** to confirm that you want to cancel the bookmark.

Borders and Boxes

Use the **F**ormat **B**order command to add lines above or below a paragraph, to the right or left, or to box a paragraph on all sides. The lines and boxes are PARAGRAPH FORMATS: they apply to the paragraph or paragraphs you select before choosing the **F**ormat **B**order command.

To add lines or boxes to a paragraph

1. Place the cursor within the paragraph you want to format.

2. Choose the **F**ormat **B**order command.

3. Choose the **L**ines or **B**ox option in the `type` field.

   If you choose **L**ines, choose **Y**es in one or more of the `above`, `below`, `right`, and `left` fields.

4. In the `line style` field, press **F1** to choose from **N**ormal, **B**old, **D**ouble, or **T**hick.

   Note: Your printer must support the IBM extended character set to print double, bold, or thick lines or boxes.

5. In the `background shading` field, press **F1** to choose the amount of background shading you want.

6. Carry out the command.

To remove lines or boxes (from a paragraph)

1. Select the paragraph containing the line or box format.

2. Choose the **F**ormat **B**order command.

3. Choose None in the `type` field.

4. Carry out the command.

Canceling Commands

To cancel any command before you carry it out, press Esc or click both mouse buttons within the command area. To reverse the effects of many commands, choose Undo (see UNDO for more information).

Character Emphasis

You can format characters with a distinctive emphasis, such as italic or boldface, as you type or after you type.

To format character emphasis as you type

1. Position the cursor where you want the text to appear.

2. Use the speed key shortcut, such as Alt-B or Alt-U.

3. Type the text.

4. When you are finished typing the text you want to emphasize, press Alt-space bar.

To format character emphasis after you type

1. Select the text you want to format.

2. Use the speed key shortcut, such as Alt-B or Alt-U.

To remove character emphasis from formatted text

1. Select all the text that contains the format you want to remove.

2. Press Alt-space bar.

If you are using fonts other than your printer's default font, cancel the emphasis by choosing the Format Character command and selecting the No option in the appropriate field.

Character Formats

Character formats include CHARACTER EMPHASIS (such as boldface, italic, and underlining), CHARACTER POSITION (subscript, superscript, or normal), and FONTS (type style, such as Pica, Elite, or Helvetica). Character formats can affect any unit of text, from one character to an entire document.

You can choose character formats in two ways: using the Format Character command or the SPEED KEY SHORTCUTS. After you choose a character format and start typing, Word continues to use it until you cancel the format by pressing Alt-space bar. If you have already formatted text with character formatting, you can cancel the format by selecting the text and pressing Alt-space bar.

Note: When you press Alt-space bar, Word cancels all the character formats you have chosen. If you want to cancel one format (such as emphasis), but not another (such as font), use Format Character instead. See also FONTS.

Character Position

You can format characters so that they are positioned above the line (superscript), on the line (normal), or below the line (subscript).

To superscript or subscript characters as you type

1. Press Alt-equal (Alt-=) to superscript characters or Alt-hyphen to subscript them.

2. Type the character or characters.

3. Press Alt-space bar to cancel superscript or subscript and to return to normal position formatting.

To superscript or subscript characters after you type

1. Select the character or characters you want to superscript or subscript.

2. Press **Alt-equal** (Alt-=) to superscript characters or **Alt-hyphen** to subscript them.

If you are formatting just one character, use the command twice.

Choosing Commands

To choose a command means to select an option from a command menu or submenu so that you can make further choices. To carry out a command means to confirm the choices you have made and return to your work. You can choose commands in several ways. To carry out a command after choosing options, just press **Enter** or click the command name. To cancel the options you have chosen without carrying them out, just press **Esc** or click both mouse buttons simultaneously.

To choose commands with the keyboard

1. Press **Esc** to enter the command mode.

2. Use the **space bar**, **tab**, or **right-arrow** key to move the highlight to the right in the command menu; use the **backspace** or **left-arrow** keys to move to the left. If you want, use the **down-** or **up-arrow** keys to move the highlight directly to the next line in the command menu.

3. After you have highlighted the desired command, press **Enter**.

4. If a submenu appears, use the techniques given in Step 2 to highlight the command you want.

5. When the command menu appears, use the arrow keys to select the command field you want to modify. Alternatively, use the **Tab** key to move right and down in the command menu, and use **Shift-Tab** to move left and up.

6. If the command field you want to modify contains named options, such as Yes or No, use the **space bar** or **backspace** key to highlight the option you want. If you must supply the information yourself, check the message line to see whether you can press **F1** to see a list of available options. If so, press **F1** and choose an option from the list.

7. Press **Enter** to carry out the command. To cancel the command, press **Esc**.

To choose commands by typing the command's capitalized letter

1. Press **Esc** to enter the command mode.

2. Type the capitalized letter of the command. If you are choosing the **F**ormat command, for instance, type **F** (either uppercase or lowercase).

3. If a submenu appears, type the appropriate letter of the option you want. To select the **C**haracter option in the **F**ormat command's submenu, for instance, type **C**.

4. If a command menu appears, as is the case with most commands, you will have to use the **Tab**, **Shift-Tab**, or **arrow keys** to select the command field you want.

5. If the command field contains a list of options, and if the options contain capital letters (such as Yes or No), you can choose the option again by typing the capital letter of that option. To choose the Yes option in a command field, for instance, type **Y**.

6. To carry out the command, press **Enter**. To cancel the command, press **Esc**.

To choose commands with the mouse

1. Point to the command you want to choose and click the left mouse button.

2. If a submenu appears, point to the option you want and click the left mouse button.

3. When the command menu appears, point to a command field and click the left button on the option you want. If you must type in a response,

click on the field and enter your response (or press
F1 and click on the option you want from the list
that appears). Select additional options in the same
way.

4. When you are finished choosing options, click the
command name. To cancel the command, click both
buttons at the same time.

Clearing Documents

When you want to clear a window to begin a new
document, use the Transfer Clear Window command.

To clear the screen and load a new, blank document

1. Choose the Transfer Clear Window command.

2. If you see the message `Enter Y to save`
`changes to document, N to lose`
`changes, or Esc to cancel,` decide
whether you want to save the current document or
abandon it. To save it, press **Y**. To abandon it,
press **N**.

Clearing Word

As you work with Word, the program constructs
temporary files and uses increasing amounts of free
memory. Eventually, you will see the `SAVE` indicator on
the status line. At this point, you must save your work to
continue. If the `SAVE` light does not disappear after you
save your work, you must clear Word using the Transfer
Clear All command. This command removes all
temporary files, clears Word's memory, and restores the
program to its state when you load it from DOS. You
will then have to reload your document.

Color

If you have a color monitor, you can choose distinctive colors for many screen elements and character formats.

To customize screen colors

1. Choose the **O**ptions command, select the `colors` field, and press **F1**.

2. When the colors menu appears, use the arrow keys or the mouse to select the display feature you want to customize.

3. To use one of the colors displayed on the top line, press the capitalized letter of that color. Alternatively, press **PgUp** or **PgDn** to go through the gamut of color options.

4. When you have chosen a color, use the arrow keys or the mouse to select another field.

5. Repeat Steps 2 through 4 until you have finished customizing all the display features you want to change.

6. Carry out the command.

Word saves your choices so that they are available the next time you use the program.

Columns

You can create multiple columns with Microsoft Word in two ways:

- Type **2** or a larger number in the number of columns field of the **F**ormat **D**ivision **L**ayout command menu. The **F**ormat **D**ivision **L**ayout method creates newspaper-style columns. The text in each column is independent and the positioning of the columns relative to one another is decided by page size and formatting. For information on creating columns using this method, see SNAKING COLUMNS.

- Format paragraphs side-by-side by choosing the Yes option in the `side-by-side` field of the Format Paragraph menu. This method links pairs of paragraphs. Paragraph 1 is always printed left of Paragraph 2, Paragraph 3 is always printed left of Paragraph 4, and so on. You can format up to 16 pairs of paragraphs using this method. For information on creating columns this way, see SIDE-BY-SIDE PARAGRAPHS.

Command Area

The Word 5 screen contains two general areas, the document window (enclosed by the rectangular window border) and the command area (the four lines below the rectangle).

The command menu, which is positioned below the document window, lists the commands you can use with Word. To activate the command menu, press the Esc key. Now the command menu is active, and Word is in the command mode; it is ready to act on the commands you select. You can tell when the command menu is active because (1) one of the command names is highlighted and (2) a brief description of the highlighted command appears on the message line, the next-to-last line on the screen.

The status line contains important information about Word and about the document on which you are working.

Page and Column Indicators

The page number indicator shows the document page number within which the cursor is positioned. The column indicator shows the horizontal position of the cursor on the 80-column screen. You can add a line number indicator. See LINE NUMBERS for more information.

Scrap

Indicated by two curly brackets ({ }), the Scrap is a temporary storage place for the most recently deleted or copied text. See SCRAP.

SAVE Indicator

When the SAVE indicator comes on, save your documents, glossaries, and style sheets immediately by choosing the Transfer Save All command.

Key Status Indicator

This indicator is blank unless you have pressed one of Word's toggle keys such as **Caps Lock** or **F6**. These keys are called toggle keys because you press the same key to toggle an operating mode on or off. After pressing one of these keys, a code (such as CL or OT) appears, warning you that Word is in a special operating mode. In the CL mode, for instance, all the letter keys you press will be entered as capitals. To cancel one of these modes, just press the key or use the command again. For instance, if you have pressed **Caps Lock** and you are in the CL mode, just press the **Caps Lock** key again and the CL code will disappear. For a list of the codes, see KEY STATUS INDICATOR CODES.

Copying Formats

When you create a document with complex formats, you frequently will find yourself entering a format two or more times. If you have a mouse, you can save time by copying a format you have already entered rather than keying it in again. If you do not have a mouse, you can use an undocumented technique to copy paragraph formats.

To copy a character format with the mouse

1. Select the characters to be formatted.

2. Point to a character that already has the format you want.

3. Hold down the **Alt** key and click the left button on the mouse.

To copy a paragraph format with the mouse

1. Place the cursor in the paragraph containing the format you want to copy.

2. Move the pointer to the selection bar next to the paragraph you want to format.

3. Hold down the **Alt** key and click the right button on the mouse.

To copy a paragraph format with the keyboard

1. Make the paragraph marks visible by choosing the **P**artial or **A**ll options in the `show nonprinting symbols` field of the **O**ptions command.

2. Select the paragraph mark you want to copy.

3. Use the **C**opy command and press **Enter** to copy the mark to the Scrap.

4. Position the cursor where you want the mark to appear, or if the text you want to format already exists, position the cursor directly on the text's paragraph mark.

5. Use the **I**nsert command or press **Ins**.

   The mark you have just inserted pushes the cursor down to the next line, so you will have to move back up to use the new format you've inserted.

6. Press the **left**- or **up-arrow** key to move the cursor back to the mark you just inserted, and begin typing.

Copying Text

You can use the **C**opy command and the SCRAP to copy text you have already created, and insert it elsewhere in the same document (or another one). You can also use the Repeat (**F4**) key to repeat the keystrokes you just entered.

To copy text with the keyboard

1. Select the text you want to copy.

2. Choose the Copy command and press Enter to copy the text to the Scrap. Alternatively, use the Alt-F3 speed key shortcut.

3. Move the cursor to the text's new location.

4. Choose the Insert command or press Ins.

To copy text with the mouse

1. Select the text you want to copy.

2. Move the pointer to the text's new location.

3. Hold down the Shift key and click the left button.

To repeat text using the F4 key

1. Designate the beginning of the text to be copied by repositioning the cursor.

2. Type the text you want to copy.

3. Reposition the cursor where you want the copied text to appear.

4. Press F4.

Cross-References

A cross-reference is an in-text reference to another part of the same document, such as "See the discussion on artichokes, page 16." If you define text as a bookmark, you can cross-reference it elsewhere in the document. When you print your document, Word will automatically fill in the page on which the cross-referenced text is printed.

To cross-reference the page number on which a bookmark appears

1. Select the text you want to cross-reference.

2. Choose the Format bookmarK command and type a name for the bookmark.

3. Carry out the command.

4. Move the cursor to the place you want the cross-reference to appear.

5. Type the cross-reference code **page:** (don't forget the colon) followed by the bookmark name.

6. *Important*: Press **F3**.

Word surrounds the cross-reference code in parentheses. If you do not press **F3**, Word will not print the page number.

Cursor Movement and Scrolling

Unlike most word processing programs, Word does not distinguish rigidly between cursor movement (repositioning the cursor on the screen) and scrolling (changing the display window's position relative to the text displayed). If a cursor movement key repeats, it will scroll the screen when the cursor reaches a window border. And most scrolling commands, such as **PgUp** and **PgDn**, also reposition the cursor.

If you press the **Scroll Lock** key, you tighten the link between cursor movement and scrolling. With Scroll Lock on, for instance, pressing the **up-arrow** key scrolls up one line as it moves the cursor up, regardless of the cursor's position on the screen (with Scroll Lock off, the up arrow does not scroll the screen until the cursor reaches the top window border). If you press **Scroll Lock**, however, you disable the left- and right-arrow keys if the line lengths do not exceed the window width.

Note: When the Scroll Lock mode is on, you see the code SL in the key status indicator.

The only way to scroll the screen without repositioning the cursor is to scroll with the mouse. See SCROLLING WITH THE MOUSE for more information.

Keys for Moving the Cursor

Key	Cursor Movement
Up arrow*	Moves up one line
Down arrow*	Moves down one line
Left arrow*	Moves left one column
Right arrow*	Moves right one column
Home	Moves to beginning of line
End	Moves to end of line
PgUp*	Moves one screen up
PgDn*	Moves one screen down
Ctrl-Home	Moves to top of window
Ctrl-End	Moves to bottom of window
Ctrl-right arrow*	Moves to next word
Ctrl-left arrow*	Moves to preceding word
Ctrl-up arrow*	Moves to preceding paragraph
Ctrl-down arrow*	Moves to next paragraph
Ctrl-PgUp	Moves to beginning of document
Ctrl-PgDn	Moves to end of document

Key repeats action when held down

Cursor Movement Keys with Scroll Lock On

Key	Effect with Scroll Lock on
Up arrow	Moves cursor up and scrolls up simultaneously
Down arrow	Moves cursor down and scrolls down simultaneously
Left arrow	Moves cursor left one-third window**
Right arrow	Moves cursor right one-third window**

**Horizontal scrolling works only if the line lengths exceed the window width.*

Customizing the Screen

You can customize Word's screen to suit your needs.
You can hide the command menu to see more text, as
well as the window borders, producing a "clean screen"
effect. You can, and should, display PARAGRAPH
MARKS so that you can see where you have pressed
Enter (doing so helps you avoid deleting the marks
accidentally). You can also choose to see precisely
where Word will break lines.

To hide the command menu

1. Choose the **O**ption command and highlight the
   `show menu` command field.

2. Choose the **N**o option.

3. Carry out the command.

To hide the window borders

1. Choose the **O**ption command and highlight the
   `show borders` command field.

2. Choose the **N**o option.

3. Carry out the command.

To display paragraph marks

1. Choose the **O**ption command and highlight the
   `show nonprinting symbols` command
   field.

2. Choose the **P**artial or **A**ll option.

3. Carry out the command.

To view line breaks as they will print

1. Choose the **O**ption command and highlight the
   `show line breaks` command field.

2. Choose the **Y**es option.

3. Carry out the command.

Note: If you are using proportionally-spaced type or
fonts smaller than 10 points, you may not be able to see
the whole line in the document window. For this reason,

you probably will prefer to choose the No option in the
`show line breaks` field when using such fonts.
Toggle the line break display on and off using **Alt-F7**.

Date and Time

Using the permanent glossary entries, you can enter the
System date and time in your documents. Word will
insert the date and time in your document on-screen or,
if you want, at the time of printing.

To make use of these features, you must set the date and
time on your system using the DOS commands DATE
and TIME. If you have a clock/calendar board, the date
and time will be set automatically when you start your
system.

To control the format in which dates and times are inserted

1. Position the cursor where you want the date or time
   to appear.

2. Choose the Options command.

3. Choose the date (Month/Day/Year or Day/Month/
   Year) and time formats (12 or 24 hours) you prefer
   in the `date format` and `time format`
   fields.

4. Carry out the command.

To insert the current date or time into your document using the Insert command

1. Position the cursor where you want the date or time
   to appear.

2. Choose the Insert command and, when the `from`
   field appears, press **F1**.

3. When the list appears, use the arrow keys to select
   the `date` or `time` option, and carry out the
   command by pressing **Enter**.

To insert the current date or time into your document using the F3 key

1. Type the glossary's name, date or time.

2. Press **F3**.

To print the current date or time at the actual time of printing

1. Position the cursor where you want the date or time to appear.

2. Use the **I**nsert command or the **F3** key to retrieve the `timeprint` or `dateprint` glossaries.

3. Print your document with the **P**rint **P**rinter command.

Default Directory

With Word, the default directory is where Word will store and retrieve files (including documents, style sheets, and glossaries) unless you specifically override the default. If the current default directory is C:\MSWORD\REPORTS, for example, Word will use that directory for file retrieval and saving (you can override this setting, however, by typing additional path information when you use the **T**ransfer **L**oad or **T**ransfer **S**ave commands).

You can set the default directory in two ways:

- Choose the **T**ransfer **O**ptions command and type a directory name in the `setup` command field. You can make this setting the default for all sessions by choosing the **Y**es option in the `save between sessions` field.

- If you have not saved a default directory using the **T**ransfer **O**ptions command, the default directory is the one from which you start Word.

You can start Word in a directory other than the one Word is in if you include a path statement in your AUTOEXEC.BAT file. Setup creates such a statement automatically. If you use Setup to install Word, you can

start Word from any disk or directory, and that disk or
directory will be the default.

When you make a document directory the default
directory, you need not type path information when you
store or retrieve files. Moreover, Word automatically
uses the version of NORMAL.STY, Word's default
style sheet, found in the default directory. Knowing this,
you can create several document directories, each with
its own, customized version of the NORMAL.STY style
sheet. For more information, see STYLE SHEETS and
AUTOMATIC STYLES.

Default Formats

Word will use default formats unless you specifically
instruct the program otherwise. By default, Word will
paginate documents so that they print with 1-inch top
and bottom margins, and 1.25-inch left and right
margins, on 8.5- by 11-inch paper. Word will use your
printer's default font, which is usually a fixed-width,
12-point font. It will not print page numbers.

Word's Default Formats

Format	Setting
Emphasis	None
Font	Printer's standard (such as Pica or Courier, 12-point, fixed-width)
Footer position	0.5 inch from top of page
Footnote reference mark	Normal position, default font
Footnote text format	Standard paragraph format (single-spaced, flush-left alignment)
Header position	0.5 inch from top of page
Line height	12 points (6 lines to an inch)
Measurement format	Inches

Page number location	7.25 inches from left, 0.5 inch from top
Page numbers	Default font
Page numbers	Off (no page numbers printed)
Page size	8.5 by 11 inches
Paragraphs	Single-spaced, flush-left alignment
Tabs	Every 0.5 inches

To change default formats

Use formatting commands to change the formats in one document. You can change most of these formats using the Format commands or their speed key equivalents (see SPEED KEY SHORTCUTS).

Create new defaults for all documents. You can create and save a new default tab width and measurement format using the Options command, and you can set and save new default margins using the Format Division Margins command. To create new defaults for the other styles, see AUTOMATIC STYLES.

Deleting Text

Commands for deleting text act on the selection. If the cursor is positioned on a character, that character is selected. If you have highlighted a larger unit of text using selection techniques, the deletion command acts on the entire selection (see SELECTING TEXT).

Most text-deletion commands route the deletion to the SCRAP, where they are stored until you copy or cut new text to it (the Scrap holds only one unit of text at a time). You can use the Insert command or the Ins key to insert the Scrap's contents anywhere in the document or in another document.

Keys and Commands
for Deleting Text

Key or command	Effect
Backspace	Deletes character left of cursor
Del	Deletes character on which cursor is positioned or deletes selection; routes deletion to Scrap
Delete command	Deletes character on which cursor is positioned or deletes selection; routes deletion to Scrap (proposed response) or to a glossary you specify
Shift-Del	Deletes character on which cursor is positioned *without* routing deletion to Scrap
Shift-Ins	Replaces selection with contents of Scrap

Division Breaks

With Word, you may divide your document into divisions by creating a division break. When you create a division break, Word will do the following:

- Collect all the endnotes for a division when you print, and place them at the end of the division.

- Restart the footnote and endnote numbering sequence. After the division break, the first footnote you insert will be numbered 1, even if there are many footnotes in the first division.

- Cancel all running heads. If you want the second division to have running heads, you must insert new running head entries after the division break.

- Create a page break (default setting). If you want, you can suppress the page break, or instruct Word to break the page so that the new division starts on a new column (for multiple-column text) or on an odd-numbered or even-numbered page.

All these features enable you to create a single document with separate chapters. If you break the chapters with division breaks, Word will collect all the endnotes for the chapter and print them at the end of the chapter. You must format each division so that Word starts the new chapter on an odd-numbered page. Each division can have its own running heads with short versions of the chapter's title, as appropriate.

When you create a division break, use the Format Division Layout command to control how Word breaks pages at the break. By default, Word starts a new page. But you can instruct Word to keep printing continuously, without starting a new page, or to start the new page on the next even page or odd page. You can also choose to break the page at the next column break, if you are using multiple COLUMNS.

After you create the division break, Word automatically uses the division formats in effect for both divisions. To change these formats, position the cursor in the division you want to format and choose one of the Format Division commands.

To create a division break

1. Place the cursor where you want the break to occur.

2. Press **Ctrl-Enter**.

To delete a division break

1. Select the division mark.

2. Press **Del**.

To control the page break at the division break

1. Place the cursor in the division you want to format.

2. Choose the Format Division Layout command.

3. Choose an option in the `division break` field.

4. Carry out the command.

Division Marks

After you make a choice in one of the Format Division command's menus, Word inserts a division mark in your document. This mark, a double row of dots across the screen, appears at the end of your document, just above the end-of-file mark. You will see the division mark no matter which option you choose in the `show nonprinting symbols` field of the Options command menu.

Division marks are similar to PARAGRAPH MARKS—they "store" the formats you choose. If you accidentally delete a division mark while editing at the end of your document, choose the Undo command.

Document Disk Full

If you see this message, you are probably using a two-floppy system and you have filled up your disk. The following are your options:

- Use the Transfer Delete command. When the command menu appears, press F1 to see a list of files. Use the arrow keys to highlight the name of a file you do not want to keep, and press Enter (if you have saved many documents to this disk, try deleting some old .BAK files). Then try saving your document again.

  Note: You cannot delete any file that Word has consulted during the current editing session.

- Remove the disk that is full and insert a formatted disk that has some room on it. You will need to swap disks in and out, but this procedure is necessary to avoid losing your work.

- If you do not have a formatted disk, use the Library Run command to format one. Remove your document disk and insert the blank, unformatted disk in drive B. When the Library Run command menu appears, press Enter to accept the proposed response and command, which will give you the DOS system prompt. Then press Enter to carry out the command. When you see the message prompting you to switch disks, insert your DOS disk in drive A. Then format your disk using the DOS FORMAT B: command. After the formatting is complete, put your Word program disk back in drive A, press any key to return to Word, and save your work. You will have to swap disks in and out of drive B.

Document Linking

The best way to create BOILERPLATES with Word 5 is to store the boilerplate text as a separate Word document. To insert the boilerplate text in your document, use the Library Link Document command.

Note: This technique differs from using the Transfer Merge command. When you use Transfer Merge, Word actually imports the other document's text at the cursor's location. When you use Library Link Document, however, Word inserts a hidden-text command in your document. This command tells Word to import the other document's text at the time of printing. For this reason, you can be sure that your document will always contain the latest version of the boilerplate text.

To import standard text from another Word document

1. Place the cursor where you want the imported text to appear.

2. Choose the Library Link Document command.

3. When the command menu appears, type the name of the file that contains the boilerplate text stored as bookmarks.

4. Carry out the command.

Document Retrieval

This command provides Word users with a complete
file-management system. You can use it to search for
documents anywhere on your hard disk, load them, and
print them. With Version 5.0, you can use this command
to create backup copies of your files.

To use Document-retrieval

Choose the **L**ibrary **D**ocument-retrieval command.

By default, **D**ocument-retrieval searches the DEFAULT
DIRECTORY.

To search for documents in another directory

1. Choose the **Q**uery command in the **D**ocument-
   retrieval menu.

2. Type a new pathname (such as **\MSWORD
   \REPORTS**) in the `path` command field.

If the search retrieves so many documents that it's
difficult to read the screen, narrow the search.

Note: The following search-narrowing techniques work
only if all system users have filled out SUMMARY
SHEETS correctly. The only exceptions are searches
involving dates, which Word inserts automatically.

To search for all documents by one author

1. Choose the **Q**uery command.

2. Type the author's name in the `author` field.

3. Carry out the command.

To search for all documents created before a certain date

1. Choose the **Q**uery command.

2. Type a less than operator (<) in the `creation
   date` or `revision date` field and type a
   date, using the format you chose in the **O**ptions
   menu (the default format is Month/Day/Year, as in
   2/20/89).

3. Carry out the command.

To search for all documents created after a certain date

1. Choose the Query command.

2. Type a greater than operator (>) in the `creation date` or `revision date` field and type a date, using the format you chose in the Options menu (the default format is Month/Day/Year).

To change the way Document-retrieval displays the document list

1. After displaying a list of documents with Library Document-retrieval, press Esc to enter the command menu.

2. Choose the View option.

3. When the submenu appears, choose the Full or Long options.

4. Carry out the command.

The Full option displays document titles as well as file names. The Long option displays the document summary sheet for the highlighted document.

If you choose the Full option, you can change the information that is displayed by using the `Sort by` field in the View menu. If you select Creation-date, for example, Word will sort the list by creation date and display this date in addition to the title.

For information on backing up and archiving your work with Document-retrieval, see BACKING UP YOUR WORK.

Edit Command Menu

When you start Word, you see the document window and the edit command menu. Here is a quick overview of the commands on this menu:

Copy	Copies selected text to Scrap or glossary
Delete	Deletes selected text to Scrap or glossary

Format	Formats characters, paragraphs, and page styles; adds footnotes, annotations, bookmarks; searches and replaces styles throughout document
Gallery	Creates and edits style sheets
Help	Obtains on-line help
Insert	Inserts text from Scrap or from glossary
Jump	Jumps to a page, footnote, annotation, or bookmark
Library	Miscellaneous commands for sorting, retrieving documents, hyphenating, linking to spreadsheets, using DOS, using Thesaurus, using Spell, and so on
Options	Sets window and general operating options
Print	Prints document to file or printer; repaginates document and previews before printing
Quit	Quits Word and returns to DOS
Replace	Replaces text throughout document
Search	Searches for specified text
Transfer	All file operations: loads, saves, clears, merges, deletes, renames documents and glossaries
Undo	Restores file to state prior to last command or editing change
Window	Splits, closes, or moves window

Fonts

If your printer can use more than one style and size of type, Word can take advantage of its capabilities. You assign styles and sizes using the font name and font size

fields of the Format Character menu. Font formats are
CHARACTER FORMATS, and you enter them—and
remove them—just as you would any other character
formats.

Unless specified otherwise, Word uses the default font
for your printer. This font is usually a 12-point, fixed-
width font such as Pica or Courier.

A common problem when using a font other than the
default is that the default font appears on your printout.
This happens because when you press **Alt-space bar** to
cancel other character formats, such as emphasis, Word
cancels the special fonts you have chosen as well, and
restores the default font. Because you cannot see fonts
on the screen, this problem is common and very
irritating. To solve it, create a new default font for all
documents using an AUTOMATIC STYLE. This step is
strongly recommended if you plan to frequently use a
font other than your printer's default font.

For information on viewing your font size choices on
color monitors, see COLOR.

To choose fonts and font sizes from a list

1. Choose the Format Character command and
   position the cursor in the `font name` field.
   Alternatively, use the **Alt-F8** speed key shortcut.

2. Press **F1** to see the list of fonts available with your
   printer.

3. Highlight the font you want, but do not carry out
   the command yet. Word places the font name you
   have chosen in the `font name` command field.

4. Press **Tab** to move the highlight to the `font
   size` command field.

5. Press **F1** to see a list of the font sizes available for
   the font you have chosen.

6. Choose a font size.

7. Carry out the command.

To choose a font for your entire document

1. Do not choose a font name or size until you have finished completely editing your document. Until then, just type with the default font.

2. Press **Shift-F10** to select the whole document.

3. Choose the **F**ormat **C**haracter command and type a font name or size in the `font name` or `font size` fields (or choose from a list by pressing **F1**).

4. Carry out the command and print your document.

Footnotes

You may choose between footnotes and endnotes for each division you create. By default, Word prints footnotes at the bottom of the page, automatically "floating" excess footnote text to the bottom of the next page if it will not fit on one page. The program inserts a two-inch line to separate the text from the notes.

To place notes at the end of a division

Choose the **E**nd option in the `footnotes` field of the **F**ormat **D**ivision **L**ayout command menu. Endnotes appear at the end of a division. If your document has only one division, which is normally the case, then the footnotes will appear at the end of your document, positioned just below the last line of text.

To place notes at the bottom of a page

Choose the **S**ame-page option in the `footnotes` field of the **F**ormat **D**ivision **L**ayout command menu.

When you create a footnote, Word enters a footnote reference mark into your text. The reference mark is not superscripted. Then Word scrolls automatically to the footnote entry area, a special space beyond the end mark. You type the footnote text there. To return to the cursor's location in your document, choose the **J**ump **F**ootnote command.

You can superscript footnote reference marks and
format footnote text manually, but the easy way is to use
AUTOMATIC STYLES.

To insert a footnote

1. Position the cursor where you want the footnote
   reference mark to appear.

2. Choose the Format Footnote command. When the
   `reference mark` command field appears,
   leave the field blank and press Enter if you want
   Word to number your notes automatically.

   If you type any character, such as an asterisk or a
   number, Word will use what you have typed as the
   footnote reference mark. You can type up to 28
   characters in the reference mark field, but it is best
   to rely on Word's automatic numbering.

3. Carry out the command.

   Word echoes the footnote number in the special
   footnote area, beyond the end mark.

4. Type the footnote text.

5. To move back to the footnote reference mark,
   choose the Jump Footnote command.

   You can press PgUp or use other scrolling
   techniques to go back to the reference mark, but
   Jump Footnote takes you to the exact spot where
   you used the Format Footnote command.

6. To superscript the footnote reference mark, make
   sure the cursor is positioned on the reference mark.
   Then press Alt-plus (Alt- +) twice.

To revise the text of a note

1. Select the reference mark of the note you want to
   edit.

2. Choose the Jump Footnote command.

   Word automatically scrolls to the footnote text of
   the footnote you have selected.

3. Revise the footnote as you would edit ordinary text.

4. Choose the Jump Footnote command to return to the footnote reference mark.

Do not try to delete a note by deleting all the footnote text in the footnote area. If you do, you will see the message, `Not a valid action for footnotes`. To delete a note, simply position the cursor on the reference mark and press Del. Word cuts the footnote to the Scrap and removes the footnote text from the footnote area (you can tell when you've cut a footnote to the scrap: Word indicates its presence there using two cloverleaf characters).

To move notes

1. Place the cursor on the reference mark and press Del.

   Word places the reference mark and the footnote text in the Scrap.

2. Move the cursor to the footnote's new location.

3. Press Ins or use the Insert command.

Footnote Window

A useful Word feature for scholars, legal professionals, and others who use footnotes is the footnote window, a special window that automatically displays the text of footnotes currently displayed in the document window. The footnote window is wonderful to use while editing. As you scroll through your document, the program automatically displays the notes relevant to the text you are editing. You can move to the notes and edit or format the notes just by switching windows.

Note: You can open a footnote window even if you've zoomed a window to full size—something you cannot do with other windows.

To open the footnote window

1. Choose the Window Split Footnote command.

2. When the `at line` field appears, type the line at which you want the window split. Alternatively,

press **F1** to activate the special cursor, and press the **down-arrow** key until you have selected the line you want.

3. Carry out the command.

Word splits the screen with a line of dashes and, if there is a footnote reference mark in the document window, displays the footnote text in the footnote window. If there is no reference mark in the document window, the footnote window becomes blank.

To close the footnote window, choose the **W**indow **C**lose command and type the footnote window's number in the command field. Alternatively, click both buttons on the right border.

Note: The footnote window displays endnotes and annotations as well as footnotes. (For more information, see ANNOTATING TEXT.)

Form Letters

A form letter is a letter you send to many people. With Word, you can create a letter that contains some personalized elements ("Dear Dr. Rogers" or "Dear Mr. Lindquist").

To create a personalized form letter with Word, you create a main document, containing the text of the letter you want to send to many people. You also create a data document, which contains the data (such as names and addresses) you want Word to insert in each copy of the form letter. Finally, you use the **P**rint **M**erge command to print the letters. Word begins by printing the first form letter using the first name and address in the data document. It continues with the second, and so on.

Before you begin your form letter application, make a list of the types of information you want your form letter to include. The words you use to describe each type of information are called field names. Each field name must be a single word of up to 64 characters (you may use letters, numbers, and underscore characters).

To create a data document

1. On the first line of a new Word document, type the field names you have decided to use, separated by commas or tabs. When you finish typing the names, press **Enter**.

   This paragraph of field names is called the header record. It should look like this (if you use commas):

   LASTNAME,FIRSTNAME,SALUTATION, COMPANY_NAME,STREET_ADDRESS,CITY, STATE,ZIP

2. On the second line, type the information for the first individual in your mailing list.

   Note: You must type this information in the same order you used in the header record. Press **Enter** when you finish.

   Williams,Nancy,Dr.,University of Western Maryland,210H Jacobs Hall,College City,MD,20298

   The information for one individual is called a data record.

   Note: Every data record must have exactly the same number of commas or tab strokes as the header record. If there are too many or too few, Word will not print the record properly. Check each record to make sure that it is correct.

   If you must use commas within one of the fields of the record, surround the item with quotation marks:

   Faraday,Henry,Mr.,"Lawrence, Smith, and Jones",111 Attorney Lane,Oldtown, Virginia,22999

3. Continue adding new records, one for each individual. Do not add blank lines by pressing **Enter**. Check each record carefully to make sure that: (a) you have typed the information in exactly the same sequence you used in the data record, and (b) you used exactly the same number of commas or tab keystrokes in each data record (use quotation marks around any field containing commas).

If you do not have all of the information you need for an individual, you can leave a field blank, but do not omit the comma. If you are not sure you know the name of Henry Faraday's law firm, for instance, enter his record like this:

Faraday,Henry,Mr.,,111 Attorney Lane, Oldtown,Virginia,22999

The field for COMPANY_NAME is blank, but the record has precisely the correct number of commas.

4. When you finish typing all the data records, save the data document.

To create a main document

1. Type the letter you want to send to many people.

2. Position the cursor at the beginning of the document and press **Enter** to create a blank line.

   Position the cursor in the blank line.

3. Press **Ctrl-[** (left bracket) to enter a left chevron symbol (<<).

4. Type **DATA** and press the **space bar**.

5. Type the data document's file name (you can omit the period and extension [.DOC] if you saved the data document using Word's default extension.)

6. Press **Ctrl-]** (right bracket) to enter a right chevron (>>).

   If your data document is called MAILLIST.DOC, the DATA instruction should look like this:

   ```
   <<DATA maillist>>
   ```

7. Now position the cursor where you want the correspondent's address to appear. Type the field names you have used in your data document.

   Surround each field name with chevrons using **Ctrl-[** and **Ctrl-]**. The correspondent's address should look like this:

   ```
   <<FIRSTNAME>> <<LASTNAME>>
   <<COMPANY_NAME>>
   <<STREET_ADDRESS>>
   <<CITY>>, <<STATE>> <<ZIP>>
   ```

Be sure to leave spaces and add punctuation as shown.

8. Now type the opening like this:

   Dear <<SALUTATION>> <<LASTNAME>>:

9. Carefully check the field names you have typed. Is each spelled exactly the same way you spelled the field names in the data document? Is each field name surrounded by chevrons?

10. When you have checked your main document for errors, save it using the Transfer Save command.

To print form letters

1. Before you begin, be sure that your data document is in the DEFAULT DIRECTORY. If it isn't, use DOS to copy the file to the default directory.

2. Load the main document and choose the Print Merge Printer command.

If you see an error message when you use Print Merge, check the following:

- Did you use the correct file name in the data document? If not, type the correct file name.

- Is the data document in the default directory? If not, use DOS to place it there.

- Does your data document begin with a header record containing the field names you are using? If not, create a header record.

- Does each data record contain precisely the same number of commas or tab keystrokes you used in your header record? If not, add or delete commas as necessary. Use quotation marks if a field entry contains a comma.

- Does your data document contain blank lines? If so, remove them.

- Do your field names include unacceptable characters (you can only use letters, numbers, and underscore characters, and the field name must begin with a letter). If so, change the field names in the data and main documents.

- Did you spell the field names exactly the same way everywhere you used them?

- Did you surround the DATA instruction and all field names with chevrons in the main document? If not, press **Ctrl-[** or **Ctrl-]** to add the chevrons.

Forms

Forms are a necessary part of work routines in organizations: they remind us to provide the information others need to do their jobs correctly. With Word, you can create forms in the following two ways:

- Use BORDERS AND BOXES to create handsome-looking business forms, which you can print and then reproduce cheaply by photocopying them. People then fill them out by hand.

- Use Word's special commands to fill out forms right on the screen.

To create a periodic report form with marking characters

1. Create a blank version of the form.

2. Position the cursor where you will type the first piece of information you must supply. For instance, the first information you type in a sales report form will probably be the dates of the sales period.

3. Press **Ctrl-]** to enter the marking character (a right chevron).

4. Select the chevron and press **Alt-E** twice to format the chevron as hidden text.

5. Continue in this way, adding right chevrons (formatted as hidden text) everywhere you will type information when you fill out the form.

6. Save the document.

To fill out a form you have created with marking characters

1. Load the document.

2. Press **Ctrl->** (greater than) to move to the first data entry field.

3. Type the data.

4. Press **Ctrl->** to move to the next data entry field.

5. Repeat Steps 2 through 4 to complete the form. If you need to move back to correct an error, press **Ctrl-<** (less than).

6. Print the form by choosing **P**rint **P**rinter.

7. If you want to save the form as you have filled it out, use the **T**ransfer **S**ave command and choose a new file name. If not, choose **T**ransfer **C**lear **W**indow and press **N** to abandon your changes.

This procedure preserves the blank version of the form so that you can use it again.

Function Keys

Function Key Combinations

Key	*Alone*	*With Shift*
F1	Next window	Undo
F2	Calculate	Outline edit
F3	Glossary	Record macro
F4	Repeat edit	Repeat search
F5	Overtype	Outline organize
F6	Extend Selection	Column select
F7	Word left	Sentence left
F8	Word right	Sentence right
F9	Previous paragraph	Current line
F10	Next paragraph	Whole document

Key	With Ctrl	With Alt
F1	Zoom Window	Set tabs
F2	Header	Footer
F3	Step Macro	Copy to Scrap
F4	*Toggle case*	*Show Layout*
F5	Line draw	Go to page
F6	Thesaurus	Spell
F7	Load	*Show line breaks*
F8	Print	Select font
F9	*Print preView*	Toggle display
F10	Save	Record style

Note: New Version 5 function key assignments are shown in *italic*.

Glossaries

Word's glossaries are very much like the SCRAP, except that there are more than one of them, and each glossary has a name. You can use glossaries to store text ranging from one character to a diskfull, which you can insert at a keystroke. You also use glossaries to store MACROS.

To create a glossary entry

1. Type the text you want the entry to contain. You can include character and paragraph formatting.

2. Select the text.

   If you want the formatting of the paragraph to be part of the entry, be sure to select the paragraph mark at the end of that paragraph. To switch on paragraph marks, choose the Partial or All options in the `show nonprinting symbols` field of the Options menu.

3. Choose the Copy or Delete commands.

4. When the `to` command field appears, type the name you want to give the glossary.

   Glossary names must be one word, and cannot exceed 31 characters. You can use underscores, periods, and hyphens, although the name of a glossary entry cannot begin or end with these characters. You cannot use other punctuation and you cannot use spaces.

5. Carry out the command.

To retrieve a glossary entry

1. Choose the Insert command.

2. When the `from` field appears, type the glossary name.

   If you cannot remember the glossary name, press **F1** and choose from the list.

3. Carry out the command.

To retrieve a glossary entry using the F3 shortcut

1. Type the glossary name. Position the cursor immediately after the name you have just typed.

2. Press **F3**.

To edit glossary text

1. Insert the entry with the Insert command or **F3**.

2. Edit the text.

3. Select the text and use the Copy or Delete commands. Give the glossary entry the same name you used before, and carry out the command.

4. When the message `Enter Y to replace glossary entry, N to retype name or Esc to cancel` appears, press **Y**.

To delete a glossary entry that is no longer needed

1. Choose the Transfer Glossary Clear command.

2. Press **F1** to display the list of glossary names.

3. Highlight the name of the entry you want to delete and carry out the command. To delete all the

glossary entries you have created, leave the field blank and carry out the command.

Note: You cannot delete the entries called `page`, `date`, `time`, `footnote`, `nextpage`, `dateprint`, and `timeprint`. These entries are permanent.

4. When the message `Enter Y to clear glossary names` appears, press **Y**.

To save your entries to NORMAL.GLY

1. Choose the **T**ransfer **G**lossary **S**ave command.

2. When the command menu appears, you will see that Word has proposed NORMAL.GLY as the destination for your entries.

3. Carry out the command to save your entries to NORMAL.GLY.

To save the entries created in a new glossary file

1. Choose the **T**ransfer **G**lossary **S**ave command.

2. When the command menu appears, type a new glossary file name.

The file name must conform to DOS rules (no more than eight letters or numbers). Omit the period and extension; Word will supply the .GLY extension automatically.

Be sure to use a file name that will remind you of the file's contents.

To load a glossary file

1. Choose the **T**ransfer **G**lossary **L**oad command.

2. When the command menu appears, type the name of the glossary file you want to load.

3. Carry out the command.

   If the glossary file you want is not in the default directory, include path information as needed. If you cannot remember the name of the file, press **F1** to search for the file. When you find it, highlight its name and press **Enter**.

Graphics

Word 5's new graphics features allow you to include graphics in Word documents. You can see the graphics in Print preView, and the graphics are seamlessly integrated with text when you print them. You can size and anchor graphics, moreover, so that text "floats" around the graphics frame (see ANCHORING TEXT AND GRAPHICS).

Word 5 can read several important graphics formats directly. For those it cannot read, you can use the CAPTURE.COM utility on Program Disk 1. This utility "captures" any graphics screen image to a Word-readable file format. In short, if you can display it on your computer's screen, you can print it in a Word document. The following is an overview of the formats Word can read directly.

To import a graphic into a Word document using automatic sizing

1. Place the cursor where you want the image to appear.

2. Choose Library Link Graphic. When the command menu appears, type the graphic's file name in the `filename` field.

   If you are not sure what the file name is, press F1 to see a list of files. If you are using Windows, choose Clipboard to import a bit-mapped image from the clipboard.

3. Carry out the command.

   Word adds a message to your file at the cursor's location. The message, which begins with a hidden text command (.G.), specifies the file's name and location, the width and height of the image, and the file's format.

To add borders or shading

1. Position the cursor within the information about the graphic image that was inserted by the Library Link Graphic command.

2. Choose the Format Border command, and choose lines, boxes, or shading.

3. Carry out the command.

To add a caption

1. Position the cursor on the paragraph mark that ends the information about the graphic, and press Ctrl-Enter to start a new line. Press Ctrl-Enter again.

2. Type the caption.

3. Press Alt-C to center the caption.

The Format pOsition command provides many options for positioning the frame of the graphic or test on the page. For more information, see ANCHORING TEXT AND GRAPHICS.

To change the graphics resolution of your printer

1. Choose the Print Options command.

2. Select the graphics resolution field and press F1.

3. Choose the resolution you want from the list and press Enter.

Graphics Mode

With most video adapters, you can choose to display your document in TEXT MODE or graphics mode. In the graphics mode, Word displays character emphases (boldface, underlining, italic, superscript and subscript, small capitals, strike-through formatting, and double underlining) the way they will appear when printed. If you are creating a document that uses both underlining and italic, it is very useful to see these formats on-screen the way they will print; in the text mode, both are shown with underlining, and you cannot distinguish between them on the screen. Despite its advantages, the graphics mode is significantly slower than the text mode.

To choose the display mode, use the Options command and highlight the display mode field. Press F1 to view the list of available modes, select the text mode, and press **Enter**. To toggle between the last two modes you have chosen, press **Alt-F9**.

Hanging Indentation

You can create hanging indentations with other measurements using the **F**ormat **P**aragraph command. A hanging indentation is a format in which the first line is flush to the left margin, while second and subsequent lines (called runover lines) are indented. The trick is to place a negative number in the first line command field.

To create hanging indentations

1. Choose the **F**ormat **P**aragraph command and type the indentation for the turnover lines in the `left indent` command field.

   If you would like the turnover lines indented one inch, for instance, enter **1 in** in this field.

2. Select the `first line` command field, and using a negative number, indicate how far to the left of the turnover lines you want the first line to be positioned.

   To position the first line 0.5 inch to the left of the turnover lines, for instance, type **-0.5 in**.

3. Carry out the command.

Headers and Footers

Running heads are short versions of a document's title or other information that prints at the top or bottom of every page. A running head positioned at the top of the page is called a *header*; a running head at the bottom of the page is called a *footer*. Word's header and footer capabilities are excellent; you can create multiple-line running heads, position different running heads on odd and even pages, and insert PAGE NUMBERS in running heads.

To add a running head to your document

1. Type the running head text at the beginning of your document and press **Enter**.

2. Press the **up arrow** to position the cursor in the paragraph you have just created.

3. Choose the **F**ormat **R**unning-head command.

4. When the **F**ormat **R**unning-head command menu appears, choose the **T**op option in the `position` field to create a header, or choose the **B**ottom option in the same field to create a footer.

5. Carry out the command. Alternatively, choose the **Ctrl-F2** speed key shortcut to create a header or **Alt-F2** to create a footer.

After you carry out the **F**ormat **R**unning-head command, a caret (^) appears in the selection bar next to the running head text. The caret tells you that the paragraph will print as running head text, not as normal text.

To create different running heads for odd and even pages

1. Type the header text you want to appear on the odd-numbered (right-side) pages. Press **Alt-R** to format the text flush to the right margin, and press **Enter**.

2. Type the header text you want to appear on the even-numbered (left-side) pages. Press **Alt-P** to format the text flush to the left margin, and press **Enter**.

3. Place the cursor on the first header, and choose the **T**op option in the `position` field. Then choose the **Y**es option in the `odd pages` field of the **F**ormat **R**unning-head command menu. Choose the **N**o option in the `even pages` field.

4. Carry out the command.

5. Place the cursor on the second header, the one for even (right-side pages), and choose the **F**ormat **R**unning-head command again. Choose **T**op in the `position` field. Then select the **Y**es option in the `even pages` field, but choose the **N**o option in the `odd pages` field.

6. Carry out the command.

You can improve the appearance of these running heads by adding lines with the **F**ormat **B**order command.

If you choose the **Y**es option in the `show style bar` field of the **O**ptions menu, Word displays running head codes in the style bar. Here is a quick overview of the codes Word inserts after you use the **F**ormat **R**unning-head command.

Running Head Codes in the Style Bar

Code	Meaning
t	Top (header), odd and even pages
tf	Top (header), first page only
te	Top (header), even pages only
to	Top (header), odd pages only
b	Bottom (footer), odd and even pages
bf	Bottom (footer), first page only
be	Bottom (footer), even pages only
bo	Bottom (footer), odd pages only

Headings

You can format headings so that Word will not break a page between a heading and the text positioned beneath it. You can also create new key codes for headings so that Word will automatically create an outline as you create headings in your document.

To format headings to prevent bad page breaks

1. Select the heading.

2. Choose the **F**ormat **P**aragraph command.

3. Type the number of blank lines you want below the heading in the `space after` field.

4. Choose **Y**es in the `keep follow` field.

5. Carry out the command.

To create heading key codes that automatically appear in outlines

1. Type the format you want for the first-level heading. For example, create a centered, boldfaced heading, followed by three blank lines. Be sure to choose the Yes option in the `keep follow` field. Include a font and size if you want.

2. Select the text you have formatted.

3. Choose the Format Stylesheet Record command or use the Alt-F10 keyboard shortcut.

4. Type H1 in the `key code` field.

5. In the `usage` field, choose Paragraph.

6. In the `variant` field, type Heading level 1.

7. Carry out the command.

Create additional key codes in this way for second- and third-level headings. For the second-level heading, type Heading level 2 when you fill out the `variant` field. For the third-level heading, type Heading level 3 when you fill out the `variant` field.

Word records the modified styles in NORMAL.STY, the default style sheet. To save your modification, press Y when you quit Word and you are asked whether you want to save the changes to the style sheet.

To use the styles you created, enter them just as you would any speed key. Hold down the Alt key and press the key code.

Help

You can ask for help at any time while you work with Word. Quick Help displays informative text screens about the operation you are performing when you ask for Help. If you want, you can ask for TUTORIAL HELP, which gives you access to "Learning Word" lessons for review purposes.

To ask for Quick Help about a command

1. Highlight the command name or command field.

2. Press **Alt-H** .

To ask for Quick Help about a command with the mouse

1. Highlight the command name or command field.

2. Point to the help mark (?) on the status line.

3. Click the left mouse button.

To see a list of Help topics

1. Choose the **H**elp command from the command menu.

2. When the **H**elp command menu appears, choose the **I**ndex option.

3. When the **H**elp topic index appears, use the arrow keys to highlight the one you want.

4. Press **Enter** .

To return to your document

1. Choose the **E**xit command on the **H**elp command menu.

2. Press **Enter** .

Hidden Text

If you format text as hidden text, you can choose whether it appears on the screen or is sent to the printer. CHARACTER FORMATS include hidden text.

To create hidden text as you type

1. Choose the **Y**es option in the `show hidden text` field of the **O**ptions menu.

2. Choose the **Y**es option in the `hidden` command field of the **F**ormat **C**haracter menu. Alternatively, use the **Alt-E** speed key shortcut.

3. Type the text you want to hide. As you type, it appears with a special dotted underline, the hallmark of hidden text when displayed on the screen.

4. When you come to the end of the text, press **Ctrl-space bar** to cancel hidden text formatting.

To format hidden text after you type

1. Choose the **Y**es option in the `show hidden text` field of the **O**ptions menu.

2. Select the text you want to hide. Be sure to include trailing spaces.

3. Choose the **Y**es option in the `hidden` command field of the **F**ormat **C**haracter menu. Alternatively, use the **Alt-E** speed key shortcut.

To hide the text on the screen

1. Choose the **O**ptions command.

2. Select the **N**o option in the `show hidden text` field and carry out the command.

Word displays an arrow that points both ways where you have hidden text. The symbol is not shown, however, if you choose the **N**one option in the same command field.

To print hidden text (whether or not it is displayed on the screen)

1. Choose the **P**rint **O**ptions command.

2. Select the **Y**es option in the `hidden text` command field.

3. Carry out your command and print your document.

Hyphenating Words

If you are creating a document to be reproduced directly from Word printouts, you may want to consider hyphenating lengthy words. If you use hyphens, Word will find it easier to break lines so that the right margin is even. Hyphenation becomes more important when you are using right-margin justification and narrow column widths.

You can create three kinds of hyphens with Word:

- *Normal hyphens* (press the **hyphen** key)

   Use a normal hyphen if you always want the hyphen to appear (as in "E.E. Evans-Pritchard, the noted anthropologist"). Word will break a line, if it must, after the hyphen.

- *Nonbreaking hyphen* (press **Ctrl-Shift-hyphen**)

   Use a nonbreaking hyphen if you always want the hyphen to appear, but do not want Word to break a line at the hyphen's location.

- *Optional hyphen* (press **Ctrl-hyphen**)

   Use an optional hyphen to show Word where to break lengthy words to help even the right margin. Optional hyphens do not appear in the printed text unless they are needed to even the lines. To see where you have placed optional hyphens, choose the **P**artial or **A**ll options in the `show nonprinting symbols` field of the **O**ptions menu.

You can use automatic hyphenation to have Word insert optional hyphens throughout your document.

Indenting Text

Paragraph indents, including left, right, and first line indents, are PARAGRAPH FORMATS. You can change indent formats as often as you like in a document, but each pattern of indentation applies to an entire paragraph. You can also create a HANGING INDENTATION.

Note: Do not confuse paragraph indents with MARGINS.

To indent text from the left or right as you type

1. Choose the Format Paragraph command and type measurements in the `left indent` and/or the `right indent` command fields. Alternatively, use the Alt-N (left indent) speed key to indent the left margin or the Alt-Q speed key to indent from both the left and right.

2. Type the text. Every time you press Enter, Word repeats the alignment format automatically, so there is no need to give the command again.

3. To return to the default paragraph format (flush left, single-spaced), press Alt-P.

To indent text from the left or right after you type

1. Place the cursor in the paragraph you want to format. Alternatively, select several paragraphs using one of the variable text selection techniques. To select the whole document, press Shift-F10.

2. Choose the Format Paragraph command and type measurements in the `left indent` and/or the `right indent` command fields. Alternatively, use the Alt-N (left indent) speed key to indent the left margin or the Alt-Q speed key to indent both the left and the right margins. (There is no speed key for indenting only the right margin.)

The Alt-N speed key indents a paragraph by the default tab width. If you press it twice, you indent the paragraph by two tab widths; if you press it three times, you indent three tab widths, and so on. You can use this technique to create stepped paragraphs, in which indented paragraphs are "nested" beneath nonindented ones. If you have indented a paragraph with Alt-N, you can "de-indent" it by pressing Alt-M. Alt-M reduces the left indent by one tab width.

To create an automatic first line indent

1. Choose the Format Paragraph command.

2. Type a measurement in the `first line` field.

3. Carry out the command.

To indent text with the mouse

1. Place the cursor in the paragraph you want to format, or select several paragraphs using one of the variable text selection methods. To select the whole document, press **Shift-F10**.

   If the ruler is not displayed, click the ruler switch in the upper right corner of the window.

2. Point to the symbol of the indent you want to change.

3. Hold down the **Alt** key and the right mouse button, and drag the symbol to its new location.

Note: The first line indent symbol (|) is often superimposed on the left indent symbol ([ ) so that you cannot see it. When the two are superimposed, the first one to move is always the left indent. Then, to set an automatic first line indentation, begin by moving the left indent symbol off the first line indent symbol. Next, move the first line indent symbol to the location you want. Finally, move the left indent symbol back to its original location.

Indexing

To create an index with Word, begin by marking the terms in your document that you want Word to include in the index. Then compile the index using the Library Index command. Finally, format the index to suit your tastes or style guidelines.

You can create two different types of index entries with Word:

• *Concordance Entry*

   A word in your document that you mark for indexing. Word prints the concordance entry and prints it again in the index. Use concordance entries to mark words for indexing that actually appear in your document.

- *Conceptual Entry*

  A word you embed in the text (formatted as hidden text, so it won't print) and mark for indexing. Word does not print the conceptual entry, but it appears in the index. Use conceptual entries when the words in your document are not quite right for indexing.

You can create main entries or subentries using either technique. A main entry is printed flush to the margin in the index, and Word alphabetizes these terms. A subentry is indented and appears beneath an entry. You can create up to five levels of subentries, although one or two is usually sufficient.

To mark concordance entries automatically

1. Open a new, blank Word document, and make a list of the words you want Word to mark as concordance entries.

   Work with a draft printout of your document or display the document in a second window. Type each word on its own line, which must end with a paragraph mark. The list need not be in alphabetical order.

2. Save the file.

3. Load the document to be indexed.

4. Place the Word Utilities disk in the disk drive, and use the **T**ransfer **G**lossary **L**oad command. When the file name prompt appears, type **MACRO.GLY** and carry out the command.

   MACRO.GLY contains the macros that come with the Word program. When you type the filename, be sure to include path information if the file is not in the DEFAULT DIRECTORY.

5. After Word loads the glossary containing the supplied macros, use the **I**nsert command and choose **INDEX.MAC** from the list.

6. When you are prompted to do so, type the name of the file that contains the words you want indexed.

   When you type the file name, be sure to include path information if the file is not in the default directory.

The macro called INDEX.MAC goes through your document, marking each word that matches the list you made. Obviously, it makes sense to start the indexing process with this macro.

After running INDEX.MAC, there is nothing to stop you from expanding the index by marking more terms. INDEX.MAC simply does much of the tedious marking for you. After using it, you can use the manual techniques to mark additional concordance entries and the conceptual entries you want in your index.

To mark a concordance entry

1. Place the cursor on the first character of the word you want to index.

2. Press **Alt-E** to enter hidden text, and type .i..

3. Now place the cursor directly after the word.

4. Press **Alt-E** again and type ;.

To mark a conceptual entry

1. Place the cursor just before the text that discusses the concept you want to index.

2. Press **Alt-E**.

3. Type .i. followed by the conceptual entry and the semicolon.

Everything you have just typed should be formatted as hidden text.

To create subentries

1. Place the cursor just before the text you want to index.

2. Press **Alt-E**.

3. Type the index code (.i.) followed by the main entry, a colon, the subentry, and the end code (;).

A properly formatted subentry appears as follows:

.i.**industrial ventures:textiles;**

To create an entry that marks a range of pages

1. At the beginning of the discussion of the topic, insert an entry using the following coding scheme:

   .i.subject;

   The word "subject" here refers to the topic you are indexing. If you are indexing the topic "industry," the beginning code would look like this:

   .i.industry;

   Format the whole entry as hidden text.

2. At the end of the discussion of the topic, insert exactly the same entry that you inserted at the beginning of the topic.

3. After Word compiles your index, the page range will be indicated as follows:

   ```
   Industry 19, 43
   ```

   You will have to edit it manually so that the page range is expressed correctly:

   ```
   Industry 19-43
   ```

Summary of Options for Coding Index Entries

Appearance in Index	Coding in text
Capital investment, 11	`.i.capital` `investment;`

Industry
   capital goods, 60
	`.i.industry;`
	`.i.industry:`
	   `capital goods;`

labor disputes, 32	`.i.industry:labor` `disputes;`
luxury goods, 59	`.i.industry:luxury` `goods;`
raw materials, 19	`.i.industry:raw` `materials;`

Graphite, 19-26	`.i.graphite;`
	`[text]`
	`.i.graphite;`

mining 20	`.i.graphite:mining;`
capital 22	`.i.graphite:`
	`mining:capital;`
Manufacturing	`.i.manufacturing:`
See industry	`.i.manufacturing:`
	`See industry;`

To compile the index

1. Choose the Library Index command.

   If you want a comma and a space to separate the entry and page number, type a comma and a space in the `entry/page # separated by:` field. Modify the other options if you like. The default is to capitalize the first word of main entries and to indent subentries by 0.2 inch.

2. Carry out the command.

   Word will compile the index. For a lengthy document, the process could take several minutes.

Inserting Text

The Insert command (and its keyboard counterpart, Ins) inserts the Scrap's contents at the cursor's location. The keyboard shortcut **Shift-Insert** replaces a selection with the Scrap in one operation—in other words, it deletes the currently selected text and inserts the Scrap at the selection's location. Therefore, it saves you the trouble of deleting the text before inserting it.

Joining Paragraphs

You start a new paragraph by pressing **Enter**. When you press **Enter**, Word enters one of its PARAGRAPH MARKS in your document. To rejoin a paragraph, delete the mark.

To join paragraphs

1. Choose the Partial or All option in the `show nonprinting symbols` field of the Options menu.

   These options display paragraph marks.

2. Look for a paragraph mark at the end of the first paragraph and delete it. If you added a blank line under the paragraph by pressing Enter, you may need to delete a second mark to rejoin the paragraphs.

Note: When you delete the first paragraph mark, you lose the formatting for that paragraph. When the paragraphs are rejoined, the first paragraph will adjust to match the format of the second paragraph.

Jumping

You can move around your document quickly by jumping to a page or other location you specify.

To jump to a specific page

1. Choose the Jump Page command. Alternatively, use the Alt-F5 keyboard shortcut.

2. When the `number` field appears, type the page to which you would like to jump.

   Word's proposed response to this field is the page in which the cursor is currently positioned. To erase it, type the page number you want.

3. Carry out the command.

To jump to a specific page in a multi-division document

1. Choose the Jump Page command. Alternatively, use the Alt-F5 keyboard shortcut.

2. When the `number` field appears, type the page number followed by the division number.

   For example, to jump to page 14 of division 3, type **14D3**.

To jump to the next footnote or annotation in the text

1. Position the cursor within normal text (not on a footnote reference mark).

2. Choose the Jump Footnote or Jump Annotation command.

To jump from a footnote or annotation reference mark to footnote or annotation text

1. Select the footnote or annotation reference mark.

2. Choose the Jump Footnote or Jump Annotation command.

To jump from footnote or annotation text back to the document

Choose the Jump Footnote or Jump Annotation command. Word will return the cursor to the footnote or annotation reference mark.

To jump to a bookmark

1. Choose the Jump bookmarK command.

2. When the command menu appears, type the bookmark name. Alternatively, press F1 to choose from a list of all the bookmarks you have created for a document, and choose the bookmark from the list.

3. Carry out the command.

To jump to a position in your document using the mouse

1. Place the pointer on the left scroll bar so that its position corresponds to the portion of the document you want to see.

   If you want to scroll one-third of the way down into a document, for instance, place the pointer one-third of the way down the left scroll bar.

2. Click both mouse buttons simultaneously.

   The screen immediately scrolls to the position you have chosen, and the position indicator moves down the scroll bar to the position you have chosen.

Justifying Text

With Word, right-margin justification applies only to paragraphs you select and format with the Justified option in the `alignment` field of the Format Paragraph command.

To format your whole document with right-margin justification

1. Press **Shift-F10** to select your whole document.

2. Press **Alt-J**.

Key Status Indicator Codes

Word has several operating modes, which are toggled on and off by special keys, such as **F5**, **Scroll Lock**, and **Caps Lock**. When you have toggled the mode on, a code appears on the status line.

Key Status Codes

Code	Key/Command	Meaning
CL	Caps Lock	Letters entered as caps
CS	Shift-F6	Column select mode on
EX	F6	Extend select mode on
LD	Ctrl-F5	Line Draw mode
MR	Format Revision-marks	Mark Revisions mode on
NL	Num Lock	Numeric keypad enters numbers
OT	F5	Overtype mode
RM	Shift-F3	Record Macro mode
SL	Scroll Lock	Arrow keys scroll the screen
ST	Ctrl-F3	Step Macro mode
ZM	Ctrl-F1	Zooms Active window

Learning Word

The program "Learning Word" is an excellent example of computer-based training software. It uses short lessons to teach you the fundamentals of Microsoft Word, right on the screen. "Word Essentials," the introductory lessons, are for anyone who has never used Word. If you have no experience with Microsoft Word, you may want to use "Learning Word" before starting Word for the first time.

The "Word Essentials" disk comes in two versions—a mouse version and a keyboard version.

To use the introductory lessons in Learning Word

1. Having obtained the A> prompt, place the Word Essentials disk in drive A.

2. Type **LEARN** and press **Enter**.

3. Follow the instructions on the screen.

Line Breaks

Word does not show precisely where line breaks will occur unless you have chosen the **Y**es option in the show line breaks field of the **O**ptions menu. To find out whether hyphens will cause problems at the end of a line, toggle on the display of line breaks by pressing **Alt-F7**.

Line Draw

You can create simple, rectangular illustrations using Word's Cursor Line Draw mode. For best results, use Line Draw with a printer that prints the entire IBM extended character set.

To use Cursor Line Draw

1. Position the cursor where you want to start drawing, and press **Ctrl-F5**.

   Word displays the LD code in the key status indicator. Be sure to draw in a blank section of your document.

2. Press the **right, left, down**, and **up arrows** to draw with the cursor. Press **Home** to draw a line quickly to the left margin, and press **End** to draw a line quickly to the right margin.

3. To move the pen elsewhere on the screen, exit the Line Draw mode by pressing **Ctrl-F5** and reposition the cursor. Then use **Ctrl-F5** again.

4. To correct mistakes, exit Line Draw by pressing **Ctrl-F5** and delete the unwanted characters as you would delete any text.

To change the default Line Draw character

1. Choose the **O**ptions command menu.

2. Highlight the `linedraw character` field and press **F1**.

3. Choose an option and carry out the command.

Line Numbers

Legal documents frequently include line numbers positioned within the left margin. With the **F**ormat **D**ivision line-**N**umbers command, you can print documents with line numbers for each page, each division, or the whole document. By default, Word ignores blank lines when it counts lines. You can change this setting in the **O**ptions menu if you want Word to count blank lines. In addition, you can display the line count on the status line.

To print line numbers

1. Choose the **F**ormat **D**ivision line-**N**umbers command.

2. Choose the **Y**es option.

3. Carry out the command.

To add line numbers to your document

1. Choose the **F**ormat **D**ivision line-**N**umbers command.

2. Choose the **Y**es option.

3. Select any other options you may want. Choose **D**ivision to number lines throughout a division, or **C**ontinuous to number them throughout your whole document. Type a new measurement in the `from text` field to change the line numbers' position from the left side of the page. Type **2** in the `increments` field to print line numbers on every other line, **5** on every fifth line, and so on.

4. Carry out the command.

To control how Word counts lines

1. Choose the **O**ptions command.

2. Choose the **Y**es option in the `count blank space` field if you want Word to count all blank lines; choose **N**o if you want Word to skip all blank lines as it counts lines.

3. Carry out the command.

To display the cursor's present line number position on the status line

1. Choose the **O**ptions command.

2. Select the **Y**es options in the `show line breaks` and `line numbers` fields.

3. Carry out the command.

Note: Word displays line numbers exactly the way they will print with the **F**ormat **D**ivision line-**N**umbers command. If you choose **P**age in the `restart at:` field of the **F**ormat **D**ivision line-**N**umbers, Word will restart the line numbers at 1 after a page break. If you choose the **C**ontinuous option in the `restart at:` field, Word will number lines continuously throughout your document.

Line Spacing

Line spacing is one of Word's PARAGRAPH FORMATS. That means line spacing applies only to the paragraph or paragraphs you select before you use the Format Paragraph command. By default, Word prints lines single-spaced. If you always write double-spaced text, you can change this default by defining a new standard paragraph format with AUTOMATIC STYLES.

To double-space your text as you type

1. Choose the Format Paragraph command and type 2 in the line spacing command field. Alternatively, use the Alt-2 speed key shortcut.

2. Type the text. Every time you press Enter, Word repeats the double-spacing format automatically, so there is no need to give the command again.

3. To return to the default paragraph format (flush left, single-spaced), press Alt-P.

To double-space your text after you type

1. Place the cursor in the paragraph you want to double-space. Alternatively, select several paragraphs using one of the variable text selection techniques (see SELECTING TEXT). To select the whole document, press Shift-F10.

2. Choose the Format Paragraph command and type 2 in the `line spacing` command field. Alternatively, use the Alt-2 speed key shortcut.

Loading Documents

You can start Word and load a document at the same time. You can also load documents after you begin a Word session.

To start Word and load a document at the same time

1. Start your computer and obtain the DOS prompt.

2. Log on to the drive or directory that contains your document. If your Word documents are in the directory called C:\MSWORD\REPORTS, for instance, type

   CD C:\MSWORD\REPORTS

   and press Enter.

3. Type WORD, press the space bar, and type the name of your Word document. You can omit the period and the extension.

If you see the message, `Bad command or file name`, you need to run Setup again or modify your AUTOEXEC.BAT file so that DOS can find Word (you may be missing the path instruction that tells DOS which directories to search).

If you see the message `Enter Y to create file`, Word was unable to locate the document you named. Press Esc, and use the Transfer Load command to explore your disk.

To load a document after starting Word

1. Save your work, if you want, and clear the display window (see CLEARING WORD).

2. Choose the Transfer Load command. Alternatively, use the Ctrl-F7 keyboard shortcut.

3. In the `filename` field, type the document's filename (and the period and extension, if you used an extension other than Word's default extension).

   To retrieve the file REPORT1.DOC, for instance, type REPORT1 in the `filename` field.

4. Carry out the command by pressing Enter or clicking the command name.

Note: Word ignores lowercase and uppercase letters when saving and retrieving files, so it does not matter which you use.

When you use Transfer Load to load documents, you can press the F1 key to view a list of files on the DEFAULT DIRECTORY. Because Word 5 shows directories as well as file names on this list, you can use this command to view lists of Word files in every directory of a huge hard disk.

To view a list of files

1. Use the Transfer Load command.

2. When the command menu appears, the `filename` field is highlighted. Press F1.

3. A list of the currently available drives and directories appears.

   The names of directories below the DEFAULT DIRECTORY are shown in brackets. The parent directory, the directory above the default directory, is represented by two dots enclosed in brackets: [. .]

4. If you see the file you want, highlight it and press Enter.

To examine the contents of directories below the default directory, highlight the directory's name and press Enter. Another list of files (and directories, if there are any below that directory's level) will appear.

To examine the contents of the parent directory, highlight [. .] and press Enter. Another list of files and directories will appear. Continue exploring directories until you find the file you want.

Macros

Word's macro capabilities are extensive and powerful. You can create simple macros by recording your keystrokes. If you want, you can write much more complex macros by writing them in a Word document, using special symbols, instruction names, and programming techniques.

Note: You cannot include mouse actions in macros.

Covered here are techniques for recording macros and
for making a macro pause for user input (such as
selecting text or typing a file name).

To record a macro from the keyboard

1. Press **Shift-F3** to toggle the **R**ecord-macro mode
   on. The message RM appears in the key status
   indicator.

2. Press the keystrokes you want recorded.

   You can type letters and numbers at the keyboard
   for your macro to enter text. You can also use
   commands and speed keys. Select command
   options by their capitalized letters (usually the first,
   but not always). If there is no capitalized letter,
   choose the option with arrow keys.

3. When you finish typing the keystrokes to be
   recorded, press **Shift-F3** again.

4. The **C**opy command menu appears.

   To cancel the macro, press **Esc**.

   To save the macro, type a name. You can use up to
   31 letters and numbers, including periods and
   underscores, but the name must be one word.
   Because you will store macros in the glossary, give
   your macro name an extension (.MAC) to
   distinguish it from ordinary glossary entries.

   If you would like to retrieve the macro using a Ctrl
   key code, press the caret (^) key after typing the
   name. Then hold down the **Ctrl** key and type the
   key code you want. You can use a two-letter key
   code. The key code must not conflict with the key
   codes of macros you have already created.

5. Press **Enter** to save the macro.

To use a recorded macro

Choose the **I**nsert command and press **F1**. Highlight the
macro's name, and press **Enter**.

Alternatively, type the macro's name in your document
and press **F3**. If you saved the macro with a Ctrl key
code, just use the Ctrl key code.

To interrupt a macro

Press Esc. You can resume the macro's operation by
pressing Y.

To test a macro in Step mode

1. Choose the Yes option in the `show menus` field
   of the Options menu so that you can see what the
   macro is doing in menus.

2. Before running the macro, press Ctrl-F3 to turn on
   the Step mode.

   The message SM appears in the key status indicator.

3. Start the macro.

4. Press Enter or any other key besides Esc or Ctrl-
   F3 to step the macro through all its actions.

   You may have to press the key many times in order
   for the macro to move through all its actions.

5. Press Esc to stop the macro when you see the error,
   and press Ctrl-F3 to turn off the Step macro mode.

To make a recorded macro pause for user input

1. Record the macro following the steps just given.
   When the Copy command menu appears, save the
   macro.

2. Use the Insert command. Type the macro's name
   followed by a caret (^).

3. Carry out the command.

   Word inserts the macro text in your document
   instead of running the macro.

4. Add the following instruction where you want the
   macro to pause:

   «PAUSE Perform action and press Enter
   when done.»

   Enter the chevrons by pressing Ctrl-[and Ctrl-].

5. Select the entire macro and use the Copy command.
   Save it to the same macro name. When you see the
   message, press Y to overwrite the old copy.

Mailing Labels

You can use Word's form letter capabilities to produce mailing labels. Create a data document containing the mailing information, and create a main document showing how you want Word to print the mailing labels. (See FORM LETTERS for information on creating the data and main documents.) Then use the Print Merge Printer command to print the labels.

To create a main document for single-column, continuous-feed mailing labels

1. In a new Word document, create a DATA instruction containing the file name of the data document.

   If your data document is called MAILLIST.DOC, the DATA instruction should look like this:

   ```
   <<DATA MAILLIST>>
   ```

   Enter the chevrons by pressing Ctrl-[and Ctrl-].

2. Type the field names as you want them to appear on the mailing labels. For example:

   ```
   <<FIRSTNAME>> <<LASTNAME>>
   <<COMPANY_NAME>>
   <<STREET_ADDRESS>>
   <<CITY>>, <<STATE>> <<ZIP>>
   ```

3. Choose the Format Division Margins command, and type 0" in the top and bottom fields. Try 0.5" in the left field, and 0" in the right field. Type the label height in the page length field (such as 1.0).

4. Choose Print Merge Printer to print the labels.

Press Esc if the spacing is not correct. See FORM LETTERS if Word displays an error message.

To print labels in three columns

1. In a new Word document, type the DATA instruction and, on the same line, the field names you want to appear on the first line of the first label.

The first line of your main document should look
like this:

```
<<DATA MAILLIST>><<FIRSTNAME>>
<<LASTNAME>>
```

2. Type the rest of the field names for the first label,
   and then enter blank space after the field names.
   The blank space must be enough to advance the
   print head to the top of the next label (try two blank
   lines).

   <<DATA MAILLIST>><<FIRSTNAME>>
   <<LASTNAME>>
   <<COMPANY_NAME>>
   <<STREET_ADDRESS>>
   <<CITY>>, <<STATE>> <<ZIP>>

3. Press **Ctrl-Enter** to create a division break.

4. Position the cursor above the division break, and
   choose the **F**ormat **D**ivision **L**ayout command.

5. Type **3** in the `number of columns` field, type
   0 in the `space between columns` field, and
   choose **C**olumn in the `division break` field.

6. Carry out the command by pressing **Enter** or
   clicking the command name.

   You may need to adjust the space between columns
   measurement if Word begins printing
   inappropriately.

7. Select the set of address fields, the blank lines, and
   the division mark, and copy the selection to the
   Scrap.

8. Press **Ins** twice.

   Two copies of the set of address fields, blank lines,
   and division marks appear.

9. In the second set of address fields, change the word
   `DATA` to `NEXT`. Do the same for the third set of
   address fields.

   Be careful not to erase the chevrons.

10. If you are using continuous-feed labels, choose the
    Format **D**ivision **M**argins command. Measure the
    distance from the top of the label sheet to the first

label, and enter that measurement in the `top` field. Then measure the distance from the bottom of the sheet to the last label, and enter that measurement in the `bottom` field. Measure the distance from the left margin to the place you want Word to begin printing, and enter that measurement in the `left` field.

11. Carry out the command by pressing **Enter** or clicking the command name.

12. Choose **P**rint **M**erge **P**rinter to print the labels.

Margins

The word *margins* refers to the white space at the top, bottom, left, and right of the printed page. By default, Word prints margins of 1.0 inch at the top and bottom, and 1.25 inches left and right.

Margins should be distinguished from the paragraph indents you can create with the **F**ormat **P**aragraph command. A left or right paragraph indent adds to the existing margin. If you choose a left indent of one inch in the **F**ormat **P**aragraph command menu, Word will print two inches of blank space, measured from the edge of the page.

To change the margins

1. Choose the **F**ormat **D**ivision **M**argins command.

2. Type new measurements in the `top`, `bottom`, `left`, or `right` fields.

3. Carry out the command.

After you use this command, Word will insert a DIVISION MARK at the end of your document. Be sure to type above the mark, not below it. Only the text above the division mark will have the page style formats you chose.

To save any of the margin settings as defaults

1. Choose the **F**ormat **D**ivision **M**argins command.

2. Choose the page size, margins, running head position, mirror margins, or gutter width that you want to apply to every document you create.

3. Choose Yes in the `use as default` field.

Math

You can perform simple arithmetic operations within Word. In general, you type the expression in your document, select it, and press the Calculate key (F2). Word presents the results in the SCRAP.

To use the calculate key

1. Type an arithmetic expression anywhere in your document using one or more arithmetic operators.

   If you type numbers separated only by spaces or lines, Word assumes you want to sum them.

2. Select the expression, and press F2. The answer appears in the Scrap.

3. Press Shift-Ins.

Word replaces the selected expression with its result.

Word's Arithmetic Operators

Operator	Function	Example
+ (or no operator)	addition	8 + 5 or 8 5
- (or parentheses)	subtraction	8 - 5 or 8 (5)
*	multiplication	8 * 5
/	division	8 / 5
%	percent	10%

Normally, Word evaluates percentages first, followed by multiplication and division, and then addition and subtraction. You can alter the order of evaluation using parentheses. If you place an expression in parentheses, Word evaluates that expression first. Without parentheses, $2 * 2 + 4 = 8$, but with parentheses, $2 * (2 + 4) = 12$.

To add up columns of numbers

1. Select the upper right corner of the column of data you want to add up.

2. Press **Shift-F6** to turn on the Column-select mode.

3. Expand the selection down and right to encompass just the numbers in the column.

4. Press **F2**. Word adds up the data and enters the sum in the Scrap.

5. To insert the sum into your text, place the cursor where you want the sum to appear and press **Ins**.

Measurement Options

By default, Word measures horizontally in inches (including fractions of an inch). For the most part, it measures vertically in 12-point lines (six to an inch). You will see these measurements in the command fields of the **F**ormat **P**aragraph and other command menus. When you type numbers in these fields to change default formats, Word assumes that you are using these measurements.

To change the default measurement format

1. Choose the **O**ptions command.

2. Choose one of the options in the `measure` command field.

3. Carry out the command.

Measurement Codes and Format Options

Code	*Format*
`in` or `"`	inches (default)
`cm`	centimeters
`p10`	character positions in Pica fixed-width font (10 characters per inch)

p12	character positions in Elite fixed-width font (12 characters per inch)
pt	printer's points (72 per inch)
li	lines

Moving Text

You can move text in several ways. You can cut text to the SCRAP and insert it elsewhere. You can also cut text to a glossary and insert it elsewhere. If you have a mouse, you can move text quickly with a special mouse technique.

To move text by cutting it to the Scrap

1. Select the text.

2. Press **Del** to cut it to the Scrap.

3. Position the cursor where you want the text to appear.

4. Press **Ins**.

This technique is somewhat risky. As you scroll to the new location, you may stop to edit something you see on the way. But if you delete something to the Scrap, you delete the Scrap's contents—the text you are moving. If this happens, choose **U**ndo immediately. **U**ndo cancels the last deletion and restores the Scrap's previous contents.

To avoid this pitfall, move text by cutting it to a glossary or move text with the mouse.

To move text using a glossary

1. Select the text you want to move.

2. Choose the **D**elete command. When the `to` field appears, type a temporary glossary name (such as **MOVETEXT**).

3. Position the cursor where you want the text to appear.

4. Type the glossary name and press **F3**.

5. At the end of the editing session, press **N** when Word displays the message, `Enter Y to save changes to glossary, N to lose changes, or Esc to cancel`.

If you want to save some of the entries you have created, press **Esc**. Then use the **T**ransfer **G**lossary **C**lear command to delete the block-move glossaries and save the glossary file using **T**ransfer **G**lossary **S**ave.

To move text quickly with the mouse

1. Use the click-and-drag technique to select the text you want to move.

2. Point to the place you want to move the text.

3. Hold down the **Ctrl** key and click the left button.

Newline Command

Ordinarily, Word starts new lines automatically with word wrapping. Word fills out the line before starting a new one—until you press **Enter** to start a new paragraph. With the Newline command, however, you can start a new line without entering a paragraph mark.

To start a new line without entering a paragraph mark

1. Choose the **P**artial or **A**ll options in the **O**ptions command menu so that you can see where you used the Newline command.

2. Press **Shift-Enter**.

Because you do not begin a new paragraph when you choose the newline command, paragraph formatting commands apply to all lines separated by Newline commands. The Newline command is very useful for creating tables. Create the whole table body as a single paragraph, with lines divided by Newline commands. This way, you can select the whole paragraph for tab formatting purposes simply by placing the cursor anywhere within the paragraph.

Numbering Series Items

To get Word to number your tables automatically, you will enter a series code name (a new Word 5 feature) instead of the table number. A series code name can contain up to 31 characters, including hyphens, periods, and underscore characters, but it must begin and end with a letter or number.

To number your tables automatically

1. Press Alt-C to create a centered paragraph format.

2. Type Table and press the space bar twice.

3. Position the cursor on the second space after the word "Table," and type table: (be sure to include the colon).

4. With the cursor positioned just after the colon, press F3.

   Word places parentheses around the series code name you have just created.

5. Repeat steps 1 through 4 for all the tables in your document.

When you print your document, Word will remove the series code name and insert a number. If this table is the first table in your document, it will read Table 1.

Outlines

Word's outline mode provides another way of looking at the text you create in document mode. In outline mode, document headings appear as outline headings. You can "collapse" the text under the headings so that your document's structure is easy to see. You can even restructure your document by rearranging outline headings.

To shift to the outline edit mode and enter a Level 1 heading

1. Choose the Options command.

2. When the command menu appears, choose Yes in the `show outline` command field. Alternatively, use the **Shift-F2** keyboard shortcut.

   The page and column number indicator changes to read `Level 1`. This message tells you that the text you type will be entered as a first-level heading.

3. Now type the title of your document. If you make a mistake, use the **Backspace** or **Del** key to correct your mistake and retype the heading.

The title becomes a Level 1 heading in the outline.

To create a Level 2 subheading

1. Place the cursor at the end of the Level 1 heading and press **Enter**.

2. Press **Alt-0**.

   The cursor jumps one default tab stop right, and the status line displays `Level 2`.

3. Type the subheading.

To create a Level 3 subheading

1. Position the cursor at the beginning of the Level 2 subheading beneath the place you want to insert the new subheading.

   Use the arrow keys or the mouse to move around the outline, as you would with ordinary text.

2. Press **Enter**.

3. Press **Alt-0**.

   The status line displays `Level 3`.

4. Type the Level 3 subheading.

5. Carry out the command.

To move a subheading left (raise its level)

1. Position the cursor anywhere within the heading.

2. Press **Alt-9**.

To move a subheading right (lower its level)

1. Position the cursor anywhere within the heading.

2. Press **Alt-0**.

Note: You cannot indent a subheading more than one tab stop beyond its heading. Doing so would be illogical; every subheading should have a heading that is indented only one tab stop less.

To collapse the subheadings under a heading with the keyboard

1. Place the cursor on the heading.

2. Press **Keypad minus** or **Alt-8**.

The subheadings disappear from view, and a plus sign appears in the status bar.

To collapse the subheadings under a heading with the mouse

1. Point to the heading above the subheading(s) you want to collapse.

2. Click both buttons simultaneously.

To collapse all the subheadings down to a level you specify

1. With the cursor anywhere in your document, press **Ctrl-Keypad+** or **Alt-7**.

2. When you see the message `Enter a number between 1 and 7`, press the number of the lowest level you want to see.

To display Levels 1, 2, and 3, for example, press **3**.

To expand the collapsed subheadings one level below a heading with the keyboard

1. Select the heading.

2. Press **Keypad+**.

To expand the collapsed subheadings one level below a heading with the mouse

1. Point to the heading.

2. Click the right button.

To expand all the subheadings under a heading with the keyboard

   1. Select the heading.

   2. Press **Keypad***.

To collapse the body text under a heading

   1. Select the heading.

   2. Press **Shift-minus**.

A lowercase t appears in the style bar to warn you that there is body text hidden under the heading.

To restructure your document by rearranging headings on the outline

   1. Press **Shift-F2** to enter Outline mode, and **Shift-F5** to enter the Outline organize mode.

   2. Select the heading you want to move.

      Word deletes not only the heading, but all the subheadings and body text under it.

   3. Press **Del**.

   4. Move the cursor to the place you want the heading to appear.

   5. Press **Ins**.

Word inserts the heading, as well as any subheadings or body text under it.

To make an outline for a document you have already written

   1. Load your non-outlined document. If the document lacks a title and headings, add them.

   2. Press **Shift-F2** to start the Outline edit mode.

   3. Place the cursor in the first heading.

   4. Press **Alt-9** to define the paragraph as an outline heading.

      Word defines the paragraph as a Level 1 heading.

   5. Press **Alt-0** to lower the heading's level, if you want.

6. Repeat Steps 4 and 5 until you have defined all the document headings as outline headings.

7. Hide the body text by pressing **Shift-F10** and **Shift-minus**.

Exit the Outline edit mode by pressing **Shift-F5**.

To number an outline automatically

1. In the Outline edit mode, select the first character in the outline.

2. Choose the **L**ibrary **N**umber command.

3. Choose **U**pdate and make sure the **Y**es option is selected in the `restart sequence` field.

4. Carry out the command.

Overtype Mode

Most word processing programs have two text-creation modes: an Insert mode and an Overtype mode. In the Insert mode, which is Word's default mode, the text you insert pushes existing text to the right and down. In the Overtype mode, which you can use by pressing **F5**, the text you type erases existing text.

Note that the **Backspace** key works differently in the Overtype mode. It does not delete characters to the right, and you cannot go past the place where you began typing.

Page Breaks

You may have Word insert page breaks where you want in the text. In general, however, it is best to prevent unwanted page breaks by using the **Y**es option in the `keep follow` field of the **F**ormat **P**aragraph command (see HEADINGS). You should break pages manually only when you are sure you want a page break at all times, regardless of whether you insert or delete text above the page break.

To insert a manual page break

1. Place the cursor where you want Word to start a new page.

2. Press **Ctrl-Shift-Enter**.

To remove the manual page break

1. Place the cursor on the page break so that the entire row of dots is highlighted.

2. Press **Del**.

Page Formats

In Word, page formats such as MARGINS, HEADERS AND FOOTERS, PAGE NUMBERS, and FOOTNOTES are controlled with the Format Division command. If you enter a DIVISION BREAK in your document, you can change page formats. See DEFAULT FORMATS for information on the default settings for Word's page formats.

Page Numbers

Unlike most word processing programs, Word does not automatically print page numbers on your documents. You must deliberately turn on page numbering. You can add page numbers in two ways:

• Choose the Yes option in the Format Division Page-numbers field.

• Use one of Word's permanent glossary entries to insert page numbers in HEADERS AND FOOTERS.

To add page numbers

1. Choose Format Division Page-numbers.

2. When the command menu appears, choose the Yes option.

3. By default, the Yes option in this command prints page numbers 0.5 inches from the top of the page and 7.25 inches from the left (in the upper right corner of each page). To change the position, type new measurements in the `from top` and `from left` fields.

   To print page numbers centered at the bottom of the page, for instance, type **10.5"** in the `from top` field and **4.25"** in the `from left` field.

4. Carry out the command.

Note: When you turn on page numbers using the Format Division Page-numbers command, Word uses the default character font for your printer. You can change the font using AUTOMATIC STYLES.

To add page numbers to running heads

1. Press **Ctrl-PgUp** to move the cursor to the beginning of your document.

2. Press **Enter** to create a blank line at the top of your document, and press the **up-arrow** key to select the blank line.

3. Use the Insert command. When the `from` prompt appears, press **F1**.

4. When the list appears, choose **page** and press **Enter**.

   The word page appears in parentheses in your document. The parentheses tell you that it is not an ordinary word; it is a page number slug.

5. To format the page numbers, select the glossary entry `(page)` and choose the Format Character command. Choose the emphasis, font name, and font size you want.

6. Add text or surrounding hyphens if you want. Press **Alt-C** to center the page numbers, or **Alt-R** to format them right flush.

Note: Do not forget to format the text as running head text using the Format Running-head command.

Page Size

Word will print on virtually any size of standard paper. If you are using paper conforming to a standard other than 8.5-by-11 inches, enter new measurements in the page `length` and `width` fields of the **F**ormat **D**ivision **M**argins command menu. To choose the default for all documents, select the **Y**es option in the `save as defaults` field.

Pagination

Word 5 inserts page breaks automatically as you type. These page breaks are active; if you insert or delete text above them, they are dynamically repositioned so that you can see where Word will break the page. If you are working on a document that will not be printed with page breaks, you can turn off automatic pagination by choosing the **N**o option in the `paginate field` of the **O**ptions command menu.

Paragraph Formats

Basic to Word is a distinction between paragraph formatting and character formatting. All these formats appear on the screen, making it exceptionally easy to visualize how your text will be arranged on the page. Any time you start a new paragraph, you can change these formats. Therefore, it is very easy to create a document that includes both double-spacing and single-spacing, for instance.

Paragraph formats include:

- The alignment of text (whether it is positioned left flush, centered, right flush, or both margins justified). For more information on alignment, see ALIGNING TEXT.

- Indentation from the right or left margins, as well as the first line of the paragraph. See INDENTING TEXT for more information.

- Line spacing, such as single or double space. See LINE SPACING for more information.

- Blank lines before and after the paragraph. See BLANK LINES for more information.

Paragraph formats affect all the text in a paragraph, which Word defines as all the text you enter until you press Enter. By Word's definition, a paragraph could be just one line, such as the company's name in the letter you are writing, a heading, or an ordinary text paragraph.

After you choose a special paragraph format and start typing, Word continues to use that format until you cancel it by pressing Alt-P.

You can enter paragraph formats with speed keys (see SPEED KEY SHORTCUTS).

You can define a new standard paragraph format using AUTOMATIC STYLES. If you do, Word will make this format the default format automatically. You can add an automatic first-line indent, double line-spacing, and font formats to this style (see FONTS).

Paragraph Marks

A common complaint of Word users is that paragraph breaks get deleted during the editing process. The reason is simple. Every time you press Enter, Word inserts a paragraph mark in your document. You can edit (copy, insert, and delete) these marks just as you can any other character. However, if you use the Options command's default `visible` setting (None), you cannot see the marks. Therefore, when you are editing, you may accidentally delete a mark that divides two paragraphs, causing the two paragraphs become one.

Beware of deleting paragraph marks. The marks store paragraph formatting information. If you delete a paragraph mark, you lose all the paragraph formats you have chosen for that paragraph.

To avoid deleting the marks, make them visible by choosing the Partial or All options in the show non-printing symbols field of the Options command menu.

Previewing Your Document

With Word 5's Print preView command, you can see how virtually any format will appear in print before you waste paper and ink. Included are page numbers, running heads, page breaks, margins, headings, graphic size and position, borders, multiple column text, and side-by-side text.

Use this checklist as you preview your document:

- Do the running heads appear in the top or bottom margins? If not, you probably forgot to use the Format Running-head command to format headers or footers as running head text.

- Are there no page numbers, even though you wanted them? If not, return to your document and choose the Yes option in the Format Division Page-numbers command menu. If you entered page numbers in a running head, remember that you must insert the page number slug from the glossary using the Insert command. You cannot just type (page) as ordinary text.

- Do paragraphs appear appropriately spaced? If you are printing a single-spaced document, you may find it looks more attractive if there is a blank line between each paragraph. To insert a blank line, return to your document, select all the text paragraphs, and press Alt-O.

- If you are printing a letter, does it look balanced on the page? A letter should be positioned on the page so that the text is slightly above the center line. If the text is too high, return to your document, position the cursor under the letterhead, and press Enter several times. Narrow the margins (1.5 inches left and right) if the letter is brief; widen them (1.0 inch) if it is lengthy.

- Did you use character emphasis consistently? Have you switched from italic to underlining? To make your emphasis consistent, return to your document, and choose the Format repLace Character or Format repLace Paragraph command.

- If you are using a nonstandard font or font size, are there sections of your document where Word has inserted the normal font style or font size instead of using your specifications? Remember that pressing Alt-space bar cancels all special character formatting, including font styles and font sizes. If you are writing a document with the Helvetica 10 font, and then press Alt-space bar, Word will return to Courier 12 (unfortunately, you cannot see font style changes in Print preView, but you can see font size changes). Return to your document, select the inappropriately formatted text, and use the Format Character command to change the font.

- Does a heading appear at the bottom of a page? If so, return to your document, select the heading, and choose the Yes option in the `keep follow` field of the Format Paragraph command. Blank lines under the heading should be entered via the `space after` field of the Format Paragraph command, not with the Enter key.

You can preview page breaks with Print preView, but it is better to do so with the Print Repaginate command, which not only previews the page breaks but provides tools to adjust their placement (see PREVIEWING PAGE BREAKS).

To preview your document

1. Choose the Print preView option. Alternatively, use the Ctrl-F9 shortcut.

   Word displays the page at which the cursor is positioned. If the cursor is on page 19 of your document, you will see page 19 in the preview mode.

2. Press PgDn or PgUp to scroll through your document. Use the Jump option to jump to a specific page.

3. To leave the preview mode, press Exit. If you want, you can print your document directly from Print preView. Just choose the Print option in the Print preView command menu.

If you are not happy with the formatting you have seen, use the Format commands and make corrections as necessary.

Previewing Page Breaks

Because Word 5 displays page breaks on the screen dynamically, it is easy to see where page breaks will occur before you print. You can scroll through your document, if you want, to preview these page breaks. However, the Print Repaginate command will perform all the scrolling for you automatically, and provides useful tools for repositioning the page breaks if you see problems.

To preview page breaks with Print Repaginate

1. Choose Yes in the `confirm page breaks` field of the Print Repaginate command menu.

   Word scrolls to the document's first page break and displays the message, `Enter Y to confirm page break or use direction keys to reposition.`

2. Press Y to accept the page break. Alternatively, press the **up-arrow** key to reposition it, and then press Y.

   You can only move a page break up from its proposed position.

3. Continue previewing page breaks until you reach the end of the document.

If you entered any manual page breaks using **Ctrl-Shift-Enter**, Word will highlight the break and display the message, `Enter Y to confirm or R to remove`. In most cases, it is wise to remove the manual page break, unless you can see a good reason on the screen to retain it.

Printer Selection

If you installed Word with Setup, you chose your printer from an on-screen list; Word automatically copied the printer driver you needed and updated the Print Options menu (a printer driver is a file, with the .PRD extension, that contains information Word needs about your printer). If you want to install a different printer, you can run Setup again. Setup helps you choose the correct printer driver for your printer.

Printing

Printing the document in the active window is simple with Word. You may choose many printing options with the Print Options menu, and you can even print documents in the background as you create and edit. Additionally, you can set up a batch-printing operation to print many documents while your system is unattended.

See also FORM LETTERS and MAILING LABELS.

To print your document

1. Make sure that your printer is turned on and selected (ready to receive instructions), and that the cable is securely connected between your computer and the printer.

2. Choose the Print Printer command. Alternatively, use the Ctrl-F8 keyboard shortcut.

To print more than one copy of your document

1. Choose the Print Options command.

2. Type the number of copies you want in the copies command field (default = 1).

3. Carry out the command.

To print a range of pages

1. Choose the Print Options command.

2. Choose the **P**ages option in the `range` field.

3. Type the pages you want to print in the `page numbers` field.

Print several individual pages by separating them with a comma (**8,15,27**). You can type a range of pages using a hyphen (**8-27**) or colon (**8:27**). You can type a range and individual pages (**8-27,32,68**).

If you separated your document into two or more divisions, you must specify the page number and the division number, giving the page number first (**8D2-27D2,32D3,68D4**).

4. Carry out the command.

5. Choose the **P**rint **P**rinter command.

To print only the text you select

1. Select the text you want to print.

2. Choose the **P**rint **O**ptions command.

3. Choose the **S**election option in the `range` field.

4. Carry out the command.

5. Choose the **P**rint **P**rinter command.

To print on both sides of the page

1. Choose the **P**rint **O**ptions command.

2. Choose the **Y**es option in the `duplex` field.

3. Carry out the command.

4. Choose the **P**rint **P**rinter command.

To print in the background while you continue to edit

1. Open the document you want to print. Choose **Y**es in the `queued` field of the **P**rint **O**ptions menu, and carry out the command.

2. Repeat Step 1 to print additional documents.

3. Choose the **P**rint **P**rinter command.

Word will prepare a temporary disk file to contain the print output. Your system must have disk space available for this operation.

4. When printing begins, you can open additional documents or continue editing.

5. To stop queued printing, choose the **P**rint **Q**ueued **S**top command. To interrupt queued printing, choose **P**rint **Q**ueued **P**ause. To restart queued printing, choose **P**rint **Q**ueued **R**estart (to start the whole operation all over again) or **P**rint **Q**ueued **C**ontinue (to continue after a pause).

To print many documents while your system is unattended

1. Choose the **L**ibrary **D**ocument-retrieval command, and when the list of files appears, mark the files you want to print by highlighting them and pressing the **space bar**.

2. When you have finished marking the files you want to print, choose the **P**rint option in the **L**ibrary **D**ocument-retrieval command menu.

3. When the **P**rint submenu appears, choose **D**ocument to print just the document, **S**ummary to print just the summary sheet, or **B**oth to print both.

4. Carry out the command.

Quitting Word

It is best to quit Word by choosing the **Q**uit command rather than simply shutting off the power while Word is still on the screen. If you choose **Q**uit, Word records all the choices you have made to configure Word's operating characteristics. Moreover, the program erases the many temporary files it constructs during editing sessions. These files will clutter up your disk if you do not allow Word to erase them.

To quit Word at the end of an editing session

1. Choose the **Q**uit command from the command menu.

2. If you see the message, Enter Y to save changes to document, N to lose changes, or Esc to cancel, press **Y** if

you want to save your document. Otherwise, press **N**.

Redlining

Think of Redlining as a mode, like the Overtype mode, in which Word's characteristics change. When Word is in the Redlining mode, the text you enter appears in a distinctive character emphasis, such as uppercase, bold, or double underline, and the text you delete does not disappear. Instead, Word displays the deleted text using strikethrough characters. Reviewers have the option of accepting the changes or undoing them.

Redlining is similar to a mode, but with one exception. If there is more than one document on the screen, Word uses the mode only for the active document, the one in which the cursor is positioned. Furthermore, if you turn on Redlining, save a document, and quit Word, Redlining will still be in effect the next time you load the document. Word stores the Redlining toggle choice you make with specific documents.

To turn on Redlining

1. Choose the **F**ormat revision-**M**arks **O**ptions command.

2. When the command menu appears, choose **Y**es in the `add revision marks` field.

3. Choose the format for marking new text.

   You can choose from **N**ormal, **B**old, **U**nderlined, **U**ppercase, or **D**ouble-underlined. Choose an emphasis you are not using for other purposes.

4. To use revision bars, choose a position (**L**eft, **R**ight, or **O**utside) in the `inserted text` field.

5. Carry out the command.

The code MR appears in the status line.

To search for changes automatically

1. Position the highlight at the beginning of the file.

Press **Ctrl-PgUp** to move to the beginning of the file in one keystroke.

2. Choose the **F**ormat revision-**M**arks **S**earch command.

After Word finds and highlights the first unit of text that has been changed, the program continues to display the **F**ormat revision-**M**arks command menu. You can accept or undo the changes. To continue the search without accepting or undoing the changes, press **S**.

To remove the marks and accept the changes

1. Select the text you want to accept. To accept the changes throughout the whole document, select the entire document using **Shift-F10**.

2. Choose **F**ormat revision-**M**arks accept-**R**evisions.

   In Version 4 of Word, this command was known as Remove-marks, which did not describe its function very well.

3. Carry out the command.

Word makes the changes you have approved.

If you do not like the changes a reviewer has made

1. Highlight the changes you do not like. To undo changes throughout the whole document, press **Shift-F10**.

2. Choose the **F**ormat revision-**M**arks **U**ndo-revisions command.

Word restores the original version of the text.

Word deletes the strikethrough characters, the text your reviewer inserted, and the revision bar in the text you have highlighted.

Replacing Formats

If you have formatted an entire document with italic emphasis, only to discover that you should have used underlining, you will appreciate the **F**ormat rep**L**ace

command. This command automatically replaces one
format with another throughout your document, with or
without confirmation.

To replace a format automatically throughout a document

1. Press **Ctrl-PgUp** to move the cursor to the
   beginning of the document.

2. Use the **F**ormat rep**L**ace **C**haracter or the **F**ormat
   rep**L**ace **P**aragraph command.

3. When the command menu appears, choose **N**o in
   the `confirm` field if you want Word to perform
   all the substitutions without confirmation. Choose
   Yes if you would like to confirm each substitution.

   It is much less risky to perform this search-and-
   replace operation on formats than it is on text.
   Generally, you can use the **N**o option without risk
   of unwanted changes—but be sure that you want to
   change every instance of the format before
   choosing this option.

4. Carry out the command.

If you chose the **Y**es option in the `confirm` field,
press **Y** to confirm the substitution, **N** to ignore this
instance of the format, or **Esc** to stop searching and
return to the search's beginning point.

Replacing Text

Word can replace one unit of text with another
throughout your document, with or without
confirmation. Because the effects of this command are
somewhat unpredictable, it is best to confirm each
replacement.

To replace text throughout a document

1. Press **Ctrl-PgUp** to move to the beginning of the
   document.

   Like the **S**earch command, **R**eplace searches from
   the cursor's position to the bottom or top of the
   document. To replace text throughout your

document, therefore, place the cursor at its first character.

2. Choose the **R**eplace command.

3. In the `text` command field, type the text you want to remove.

4. In the `with text` command field, type the text you want Word to substitute for the search text.

5. In the `confirm` field, choose the **Y**es option unless you are certain of the command's effect.

6. In the `case` field, choose **Y**es to replace only the text that contains precisely the pattern of upper- and lowercase letters in the `text` field.

7. In the `whole word` field, choose **Y**es if you do not want Word to replace matching text it finds within a word.

8. Carry out the command.

Ruler Settings

The ruler contains symbols that help you understand the format settings for the selected paragraph (the paragraph in which the cursor is positioned).

Ruler Symbols

Symbol	Format Setting
|	First line indent (or hanging indent's first line)
[	Left indent from margin
]	Right indent from margin

As you move the cursor from one paragraph to another with different indents, you will see the ruler change. For information on changing paragraph indents on the ruler with the mouse, see INDENTING TEXT.

The ruler also shows the custom tab stops you have chosen for a paragraph.

Ruler Custom Tab Stops

Symbol	Tab Stop
L	Left flush tab
R	Right flush tab
C	Centered tab
D	Decimal tab
|	Vertical tab

The default tab stops are not displayed. For information on setting tabs with the mouse directly on the ruler, see TABS.

To display the ruler

Choose the Yes option in the `show ruler` field of the Options menu. Alternatively, click the left mouse button in the upper right corner of the display window.

Saving Your Work

Even if you use AUTOSAVE, you must save your document to disk if you want to preserve it for use in a subsequent computer session. To safeguard against work losses, save your work frequently (as a general rule, save every 15 minutes).

To save your document

1. Press Esc to enter the command mode.

2. Choose the Transfer Save command or use the Ctrl-F10 keyboard shortcut.

3. When the `file name:` prompt appears, type a name for your document.

   You can use up to eight alphanumeric characters, including underscores, hyphens, and the following punctuation marks:

   ```
   ! @ # $ % & ( ) ` { } ~ ^
   ```

   Note that not all punctuation marks can be used.

Omit the period and extension so that Word will supply its default extension, .DOC, automatically.

4. Be sure that the Word option is selected (surrounded with parentheses) in the `format` field. If it is not, highlight it before carrying out the command.

5. Press Enter.

6. After Word saves your document, a document summary sheet appears. Always type a long version of the document's name in the `title` field. Use two or three words to describe your document's contents; type them in the keywords field. If more than one person uses your computer, type your name in the `author` field as well. Doing so greatly facilitates document retrieval tasks. Press Enter to close the document summary sheet.

To save all open documents, style sheets, and glossaries, choose Transfer Allsave.

Scrap

The Scrap is a temporary storage area for storing text you have cut or copied from your document. The Scrap can store one character or millions, depending on the size of your disk. Note, however, that the Scrap can hold only one unit of text at a time. When you cut or copy new text to the Scrap, the old contents are erased.

The Scrap is useful for deleting text because it gives you a way to recover the deletion if you change your mind. It is also useful for COPYING TEXT and MOVING TEXT.

Scrolling with the Mouse

Keyboard scrolling commands scroll the screen relative to the text and, at the same time, move the cursor (see CURSOR MOVEMENT AND SCROLLING). The

mouse scrolling commands, however, scroll the screen
without moving the cursor or affecting the selection.

To scroll down

1. Position the pointer on the left scroll bar (the
   window's left border).

2. When the pointer changes shape (a two-headed
   arrow pointing up and down in graphics mode, and
   a big rectangle in text mode), click the left mouse
   button.

To scroll up

1. Position the pointer on the left scroll bar.

2. When the pointer changes shape, click the right
   mouse button.

You can control how much of the screen scrolls by
positioning the pointer higher or lower on the scroll bar.
The lower you position it, the more the screen scrolls.

If you have created lines longer than the document
window, you can also scroll left and right. Position the
pointer on the bottom scroll bar, and click the left button
to scroll left or the right button to scroll right.

After you scroll with the mouse, the cursor remains
where you last positioned it. If you start typing without
clicking a new cursor location, the screen will jump back
to the place you began scrolling.

Searching for Formats

You can search for formats as well as text. Use this
technique if you cannot remember where you used a
character or paragraph format that you want to change.

To search for a character format

1. To search your whole document, press **Ctrl-PgUp**
   to position the cursor at the beginning.

2. Choose the **F**ormat s**E**arch **C**haracter command.

3. When the command menu appears, choose the Down option in the `direction` field.

4. Select the format(s) for which you want to search.

   To find Helvetica text with bold formatting, for example, highlight Yes in the `bold` field and type **HELVETICA** in the `font name` field.

5. Carry out the command.

To search for a paragraph format or formats

1. To search your whole document, press **Ctrl-PgUp** to position the cursor at the beginning.

2. Choose the Format sEarch Paragraph command.

3. When the command menu appears, choose the Down option in the `direction` field.

4. Select the format(s) for which you want to search.

5. Carry out the command.

Searching for Text

As you edit, do not tire your eyes by searching for text manually. Let Word do it for you.

To search for text in your document

1. If you want to search your whole document, press **Ctrl-PgUp** to position the cursor on the first character of your document.

   Word searches from the cursor position to the end of the document (if you are searching down) or to the beginning (if you are searching up). Word is preset to search down, toward the end of the document. Position the cursor at the beginning of the document to search all of it.

2. Choose the Search command.

3. When the Search command menu appears, type the text you are searching for in the text command field.

   You can type up to 250 characters of text, including spaces.

4. In the `direction` field, choose **D**own (the default) to search from the cursor's position to the end of the document, or **U**p to search toward the document's beginning.

5. Carry out the command.

6. To repeat the search, press **Shift-F4**.

To search for an exact match of the search text's case pattern

1. Enter the search text in the `text` field of the **S**earch command menu.

2. Choose the **Y**es option in the `case` field.

3. Carry out the command.

To do a whole-word search

1. Enter the search text in the `text` field of the **S**earch command menu.

2. Choose the **Y**es option in the `whole word` command field.

3. Carry out the command.

Selecting Columns

Word's column-select mode enables you to select a vertical rectangle of text on the screen. You can copy, cut, or move the selection. You can press **F2** to sum up a column of selected numbers (see MATH).

To select columns

1. Position the cursor at the upper left corner of the rectangular column of text you want to select.

2. Press **Shift-F6**.

   The code CS appears in the key status indicator.

3. Use the arrow keys to expand the highlight to the right and down.

Selecting Text

With Word, editing and formatting commands act on the text you have selected. When you are working in a document window, the cursor is always selected. You can expand the selection (and expand the highlight) by using fixed-unit or variable-unit text selection commands. Use the fixed-unit commands when you want to select a word, a line, a sentence, or a paragraph. Use the variable-unit commands when you want to select any amount of text that does not conform to the fixed units.

Selecting Fixed Units of Text with the Keyboard

To select	*Press this key*
Character	Arrow key (**Up**, **Down**, **Left**, **Right**), **Home**, or **End**
Previous word	**F7**
Next word	**F8**
Previous sentence	**Shift-F7**
Next sentence	**Shift-F8**
Previous paragraph	**F9**
Next paragraph	**F10**
Current line	**Shift-F9**
Whole document	**Shift-F10**

Note: The function of these keys repeats when you hold them down. If the selection moves too fast, enter a lower number in the cursor speed field of the **O**ptions command menu.

Selecting Fixed Units of Text
with the Mouse

To select	Point to	Click
Character	Character	Left button
Word	Word	Right button
Sentence	Sentence	Both buttons
Line	Selection bar	Left button
Paragraph	Selection bar	Right button
Entire document	Selection bar	Both buttons

To select variable amounts of text with the F6 (Extend-selection) key

1. Place the cursor where you want the highlight to begin.

2. Press **F6**.

   The code EX appears in the key status indicator.

3. Press any key that moves the cursor to expand the highlight just as you want.

4. When you are finished expanding the highlight, choose the command you want (such as **D**elete or **F**ormat).

Most commands cancel the extend-selection mode. To cancel it manually, just press **F6** again.

To select variable amounts of text using the Shift key

1. Hold down the **Shift** key and press any key that moves the cursor.

   As long as you hold down the **Shift** key, the highlight is "anchored" at the cursor's original location, and you can expand the highlight as far as you want.

2. When you have finished expanding the highlight, release the **Shift** key.

The highlight remains on the screen. To cancel it, just touch one of the keys that moves the cursor.

To select variable amounts of text with the mouse

1. Position the cursor at the beginning of the text you want to select.

2. Hold down the left button and drag right and down to select the text.

If you drag to the window border, Word will scroll the screen.

Show Layout

New to Version 5 is the `show layout` field of the **O**ptions command menu. If you choose the **Y**es option in this field, Word displays SIDE-BY-SIDE PARAGRAPHS and SNAKING COLUMNS right on the screen—and you can edit the text while it is displayed this way. However, this option slows Word down. Use it to view your multiple-column formats, but toggle it off to enter and edit text.

To use the Show Layout mode

Choose the **Y**es option in the `show layout` field of the **O**ptions menu and carry out the command. Alternatively, use the **Alt-F4** keyboard shortcut.

To move from one column to another in the Show Layout mode

Press **Ctrl-5-right arrow** to move the cursor to the next column right; press **Ctrl-5-left arrow** to move left.

Side-by-Side Paragraphs

When you create side-by-side paragraphs, you create a two-column format in which the paired paragraphs are always kept together (Paragraph 1 on the left, Paragraph 2 on the right). If you want to create a multiple column format in which the paragraphs are not paired, create SNAKING COLUMNS.

To create side-by-side paragraphs using Word's default 6.0 inch line length

1. Type the two paragraphs with no blank line between them.

2. Place the cursor in the first paragraph. Type **3.25"** in the `right indent` field and choose the **Y**es option in the `side-by-side` field.

3. Carry out the command.

4. Place the cursor in the second paragraph. Type **3.25"** in the `left indent` field and choose the **Y**es option in the `side-by-side` field.

5. Carry out the command.

6. Press **Alt-F4** to show the side-by-side layout on the screen.

Note: You can create a maximum of 16 consecutive paragraphs with side-by-side formatting.

Snaking Columns

You can create snaking newsletter columns easily with Word, and you can mix single-column and multiple-column formats on a single page. Columns are division formats in Word. This means that the column formatting choices you make apply to your entire document, unless you break it into divisions by pressing **Ctrl-Enter**. To create a two-column format in which the paragraphs in the two columns are linked, see SIDE-BY-SIDE PARAGRAPHS.

To turn on multiple-column formatting

1. Choose the **F**ormat **D**ivision **L**ayout command.

2. Type the number of columns you want in the `number of columns` field.

   You can create up to 22 columns, although the practical limit for an 8.5 inch-wide page is a maximum of three or four columns.

3. Type a measurement in the `space between columns` field if you want to modify the default setting (0.5 inches).

4. Carry out the command.

To mix single- and multiple-column formatting on a page

1. To separate the single- and multiple-column formatting, position the cursor where you want the break to occur.

2. Press **Ctrl-Enter** to enter a division break.

3. Press the **up-arrow** key to select the division above the break.

4. Choose the **F**ormat **D**ivision **L**ayout command to select the number of columns you want, and carry out the command.

5. Press the **down-arrow** key to select the division below the break.

6. Choose **C**ontinuous in the `division break` field to prevent a page break at the division mark.

7. Type the number of columns you want in the `number of columns` field, and carry out the command.

Sorting

Use Word's **L**ibrary **A**utosort command to sort selected text in numerical or alphabetical order. The unit for sorting purposes is a paragraph. If you select several paragraphs and choose this command, Word will sort the paragraphs using the paragraphs' first number or letter.

If you want to sort material you entered with the Newline command, such as a column in a table, you must select the material using the Column-select mode (see SELECTING COLUMNS).

Speed Key Shortcuts

Word's speed key shortcuts for formatting are defined
by the default STYLE SHEET, NORMAL.STY. You
can modify these speed keys or add new ones by
modifying NORMAL.STY. For more information, see
STYLE SHEETS.

Speed Key Shortcuts
for Character Formatting

Emphasis	*Speed Key Shortcut*
Bold	**Alt-B**
Double underline	**Alt-D**
Hidden	**Alt-E**
Italic	**Alt-I**
Small caps	**Alt-K**
Strikethrough	**Alt-S**
Subscript	**Alt-minus** (hyphen)
Superscript	**Alt-plus** (+) or **Alt-equal** (=)
Underline	**Alt-U**
Cancel character formats	**Alt-space bar**

Speed Key Shortcuts
for Paragraph Formatting

Format	*Speed Key Shortcut*
Automatic first line indent	**Alt-F**
Blank line before paragraph	**Alt-O** (letter, not zero)
Centered alignment	**Alt-C**
Decrease left indent	**Alt-M**
Double-line spacing	**Alt-2**
Hanging indentation	**Alt-T**
Increase left indent	**Alt-N**
Indent left and right	**Alt-Q**

Justified alignment	**Alt-J**
Left flush alignment	**Alt-L** or **Alt-P**
Right flush alignment	**Alt-R**
Cancel paragraph formats	**Alt-P**

Spell

Version 5's much-improved Spell is faster and easier to use. Always use it to help ensure that your documents are letter-perfect, but remember that Spell cannot detect grammatical errors. If you use the homonym "wear" instead of "where," Spell cannot detect the error. There is no substitute for a final proofreading.

To check your spelling with the keyboard

1. Position the cursor where you want the spell checking to begin or select the text you want checked.

   To check your entire document, press **Ctrl-PgUp** to position the cursor at the beginning of the file. To check a selection, highlight the text you want to check, or you may select a single word.

2. Choose the **L**ibrary **S**pell command. Alternatively, use the **Alt-F6** keyboard shortcut.

   Spell begins checking the document or the selection immediately. Users of previous versions of Word will be delighted to learn that it is no longer necessary to choose the **P**roof command after the **S**pell menu appears.

   When Spell finds a word it cannot match with the correctly spelled words in its dictionary, you will see the message `Not found`, and Spell will try to locate the correct spelling automatically. If it finds a list of potentially correct spellings, it displays them.

3. To make the correction, highlight the correctly spelled word and press **Enter**. If Word cannot find the correct spelling, choose the **C**orrect command and type the correct spelling in the `command`

field. To leave the word as it is, choose Ignore.

If you want Spell to make this correction automatically throughout the rest of your document or the selection, choose the Yes option in the `remember correction` field. Choose this option, for instance, if you have discovered that you have consistently misspelled a place or person's name and need to make the correction throughout your document.

If you type a correction, Spell tries to check the correction you have typed against its dictionaries. If it cannot find a match, you will see the message, `Word not in dictionary`. Do not let this message concern you; you will get it frequently when you are correcting proper nouns or jargon. Enter Y to confirm, N to retype, or Esc to cancel. If you are sure you have spelled the word correctly, just press Y.

4. If you made a mistake or want to type the correction over again, choose the Undo command in the Spell command menu right after making the change.

5. When Word comes to the end of your document, you will see the message, `Enter Y to continue checking spelling from the top of the document, N to exit, or Esc to cancel.` Press Y if you want your entire document checked.

To check spelling with the mouse

1. Position the cursor where you want the spell checking to begin or select the text you want checked.

   To check your whole document, press **Ctrl-PgUp** to position the cursor at the beginning of the file. To check a selection, highlight the text you want to check, or you may select a single word.

2. Click the Library Spell command. Alternatively, use the **Alt-F6** keyboard shortcut.

   Spell begins checking the document or the selection immediately. It is no longer necessary to choose the

Proof command after the Spell menu appears.

When Spell finds a word it cannot match with the correctly spelled words in its dictionary, you will see the message Not found, and Spell will try to locate the correct spelling automatically. If it finds a list of potentially correct spellings, it displays them.

3. To make the correction, point to the correctly spelled word and click the right button. If Word cannot find the word's correct spelling, click the Correct command and type the correct spelling in the command field. To leave the word as it is, click Ignore.

   If you want Spell to make this correction automatically throughout the rest of your document or the selection, click the Yes option in the remember correction field.

   If you type a correction, Spell tries to check the correction you have typed against its dictionaries. If it cannot find a match, you will see the message, Word not in dictionary. Do not let this message concern you; you will get it frequently when you are correcting proper nouns or jargon. Enter Y to confirm, N to retype, or Esc to cancel. If you are sure you have spelled the word correctly, press Y.

4. If you make a mistake or want to type the correction over again, choose the Undo command in the Spell command menu immediately after making the change.

5. When Word comes to the end of your document, you will see the message, Enter Y to continue checking spelling from the top of the document, N to exit, or Esc to cancel. Press Y if you want your whole document checked.

When you add words, you may choose among three different dictionaries:

• *Standard dictionary*

   Spell always uses the words in this dictionary when it checks your spelling. So add words to this dictionary if they are likely to appear in many or most of the documents you create. Examples include your name, your street, your city (if it is not already in Spell's dictionary), names of coworkers, etc.

Note: The Standard dictionary is not the same as Spell's own dictionary, which is contained in a special, non-document file (SPELL-AM.LEX). The words you add to the Standard dictionary go into a file called UPDAT-AM.CMP. This file is an ordinary document file. If you accidentally add an incorrectly-spelled word to the Standard dictionary, therefore, you can undo the damage simply by editing UPDAT-AM.CMP.

• *Document dictionary*

This dictionary is stored with the document you are checking for correct spelling. Spell will consult this dictionary only when you are rechecking this particular document. Choose this dictionary to store correctly spelled words you are not likely to use in any other document.

• *User dictionary*

In addition to checking its own dictionary (SPELL-AM.CMP) and the Standard dictionary (UPDAT-AM.CMP), Spell also checks one additional dictionary, the User dictionary. By default, this dictionary is SPECIALS.CMP. Adding words to the default User dictionary is not much different than adding words to the standard dictionary, because Spell will check the default User dictionary every time you use the program.

To add correctly spelled words to the Standard or Document dictionaries

1. When Spell reports that a correctly spelled Word is not in its dictionary, choose the Add command.

2. When the menu appears, choose Standard to add the word to the Standard dictionary, or Document to add the word to the Document dictionary.

To create a User dictionary and add words to it

1. When the Spell menu appears, choose the Options command.

2. When the command menu appears, type a new name in the `User dictionary` field.

The new User dictionary's name must have the extension .CMP. Be sure to choose a name that describes the contents of the dictionary. If the dictionary contains legal terms, use the file name LEGAL.CMP. If the dictionary contains Karen's additions, name it KAREN.CMP.

Word saves the choices you make in the `user dictionary` field as the new default, so that Spell will use the dictionary you name the next time you start Word and check spelling again. To switch user dictionaries, start Spell and choose the Spell Options command again. Then type the User dictionary you want in the `user dictionary` field.

To cancel the changes you made with Spell, choose Undo immediately after using Spell.

Splitting Paragraphs

With Word, you split a paragraph into two by pressing Enter. When you press Enter, Word inserts a PARAGRAPH MARK. The paragraph mark indicates the end of a paragraph. For best results with Word, display the marks by choosing the Partial or All options in the `show nonprinting symbols` field of the Options command menu.

To split a paragraph

1. Use the mouse or the arrow keys to position the cursor on the character at which you want the split to occur.

2. Press Enter.

Spreadsheet Linking

You can import all or part of an Excel, Multiplan, or 1-2-3 spreadsheet into a Word document. If you change the spreadsheet later, you can update the version of the Word document easily.

To import a table

1. Place the cursor where you want the table to appear.

2. Choose the **L**ibrary **L**ink **S**preadsheet command.

3. When the command menu appears, type the filename of the spreadsheet. If you cannot remember the name, press **F1** to see a list.

   If the spreadsheet is not in the default directory, use path information in addition to the file name.

   Hint: When you press **F1**, Word displays a list of all the files in the directory. To see a list of just the Lotus files, type *.**WKS** or **WK1** before pressing **F1**.

4. Press **Tab** or click the `area` field and type the name of the range you want to import. If you cannot remember the name, press **F1** to see a list. Alternatively, type the cell range, using the same format as your spreadsheet program.

5. Carry out the command. Word imports the file.

The table that appears may not be formatted attractively. Word has ended each line with a Newline character and placed a tab keystroke between each column. Just use the **F**ormat **T**ab **S**et command, create tabs, and move them around until you are satisfied with the results.

To update the table you imported

1. Select the table. If you want to update all the tables in your document at one time, press **Shift-F10** to select your whole document.

2. Choose the **L**ibrary **L**ink **S**preadsheet command. Carry out the command without typing anything in its command fields.

3. Word highlights the table and displays the message, `Enter Y to update or Esc to cancel.` Press **Y** to update the table.

Word erases the imported table, but not the paragraph mark at the end of the table. For this reason, it does not lose the tab formatting you have assigned to the table. Then it imports the spreadsheet all over again. The new version of the spreadsheet appears, and takes the tab formatting that is preserved in the paragraph mark.

Starting Word

To start Word on a hard disk system

1. Make sure that the DOS prompt (for most systems, `C>`) is displayed on the screen.

2. Type **CD**, press the **space bar**, and type the name of the directory in which you store your documents. If you store your documents in a directory called C:\MSWORD\DOCS, for instance, type

   CD \MSWORD\DOCS

   and press **Enter**.

3. When the DOS prompt reappears, type **WORD** and press **Enter**.

Word starts and displays a new, unnamed document.

To start Word on a dual floppy system

1. Start Word with the DOS disk that SETUP modified. After you see the `A>` prompt displayed on the screen, remove the DOS disk.

2. Place the Word 5 program disk that SETUP created in drive A.

3. Insert a blank, formatted disk in drive B.

   If you are using a 360K system, you must use the document disk created by SETUP, or a copy of that disk.

4. Type **WORD** and press **Enter**.

If you are using a 360K system, you will be asked to insert Program Disk #2.

Word starts and displays a new, unnamed document.

Start-Up Options

In versions of Word prior to 5.0, you could use several switches to control Word's operating characteristics. Because the Options menu now makes it possible to control these characteristics while you use Word, the number of start-up options has been limited to those shown in the table.

Start-Up Options for Word 5.0

Command	Explanation
WORD	Starts Word and displays a new, blank document
WORD *filename*	Starts Word and opens the named document
WORD /L	Starts Word and opens the last document used; scrolls to the cursor's last position
WORD /K	Starts Word in a special mode appropriate for use with memory-resident programs such as SideKick.

Style Sheets

Style sheets accomplish three important functions in Word:

• *Modifying existing speed keys*

  If you do not like the way formatting speed keys work, you can modify them using a style sheet.

- *Creating new speed keys*

  You can create a speed key for a format you enter frequently with a style sheet.

- *Changing default formats using automatic styles*

  You can modify the default formats for page numbers, footnote reference marks, annotation reference marks, line numbers, summary sheets, line draw, footnote paragraphs, annotation paragraphs, standard paragraphs, running head paragraphs, table of contents entries, index entries, and standard divisions. See AUTOMATIC STYLES for more information.

To modify an existing speed key

1. Type some text, and use the speed key you want to modify.

   For example, press **Alt-T** to format a paragraph with a hanging indent.

2. Select the text you have formatted.

3. Choose the **F**ormat **S**tylesheet **R**ecord command or use the **Alt-F10** keyboard shortcut.

4. Type the format's key code in the `key code` field.

   To modify **Alt-T**, type **T**.

5. In the `usage` field, choose **C**haracter if the format contains character formatting exclusively; choose **P**aragraph if it contains both character and paragraph formats, or just paragraph formats.

6. Press **Tab** twice to tab over the `variant` field. Word assigns a variant number automatically.

7. Carry out the command.

Word records the modified style in NORMAL.STY, the default style sheet. To save your modification, press **Y** when you quit Word and are asked whether you want to save the changes to the style sheet.

To create a new speed key

1. When you have created a complex format you want to save, select it.

   The format can include character formatting, paragraph formatting, and custom tab stops.

2. Select the text you have formatted.

3. Choose the Format Stylesheet Record command or use the **Alt-F10** keyboard shortcut.

4. Type the key code you want to use in the `key code` field.

   Do not use a code that duplicates an existing speed key. See SPEED KEY SHORTCUTS for a list. If you duplicate an existing key code, you disable it.

   You can create a two-letter key code, but the first letter should not duplicate an existing speed key code.

5. In the `usage` field, choose Character if the format contains character formatting exclusively; choose Paragraph if it contains both character and paragraph formats, or just paragraph formats.

6. Press **Tab** twice to tab over the `variant` field. Word assigns a variant number automatically.

7. Carry out the command.

Word records the modified style in NORMAL.STY, the default style sheet. To save your modification, press **Y** when you quit Word and are asked whether you want to save the changes to the style sheet.

To attach a different style sheet to a document

1. Choose the Format Stylesheet Attach command.

2. Press **F1** to see a list of stylesheets.

3. Highlight the stylesheet you want.

4. Carry out the command.

Summary Sheets

The first time you save a document with **T**ransfer **S**ave, Word displays a blank summary sheet. Here are some tips for filling it out:

- *Title* (40 characters)

  Use this field to type a short version of the document's title, with the most significant words first (Word displays only the first two or three words of the title when you view lists with **L**ibrary **D**ocument-retrieval). If your document is titled, "Report to the Directors on the Advisability of Investing in OK Products, Inc.," type **OK Products Report to Directors** in the `title` field.

  Note: The document's title in the summary sheet has nothing to do with the document's file name. By typing a title in the summary sheet, you do not change the file name.

- *Author* (40 characters)

  It is not necessary to fill out this field unless your computer is used by more than one person. But if it is, be sure to fill it out for every document that you (and all other users) create. Be consistent—always use one spelling and one form of your name. Do not type "Dr. Margaret Smith" for one document and "Peggy" for the next.

- *Version Number* (10 characters)

  If you want to keep track of which version of a document you have saved, type a number (or any identifying text up to 10 characters) in this field.

  Note: Word does not update version numbers automatically.

- *Operator* (40 characters)

  Use this field only if you are typing a document that belongs to someone else.

- *Creation Date* (8 characters)

  Word fills in this field automatically.

If you do not want to fill out the summary sheet, press
Enter when it appears. But think twice before doing so!
Months from now, you may not be able to tell what a
file contains just by looking at that cryptic, 8-character
DOS file name.

If you have not filled out your document summary
sheets properly, or if you want to update one, use the
Library **D**ocument-retrieval **U**pdate command.

To fill out or update a document summary sheet

1. Choose the **L**ibrary **D**ocument-retrieval command.
   When the document list appears, highlight the
   name of the document containing the summary
   sheet you want to update.

2. Choose the **U**pdate option.

3. When the summary screen appears, make all
   necessary additions or changes.

4. Press **Enter** to carry out the command.

5. Choose **E**xit to leave **L**ibrary **D**ocument-retrieval.

Tables of Contents

If you are writing a proposal or report, take advantage
of Word's ability to generate a table of contents
automatically. You can create a table easily if you have
outlined your document. If you have not outlined your
document, you must mark the headings you want Word
to include in the table of contents. After compiling the
table with the **L**ibrary **T**able command, Word places the
table of contents at the end of your document, without a
page number. You insert it at the beginning of your
document for presentation.

To create a table of contents from an outlined document

1. To make sure pagination is correct, turn off the
   display of hidden text by choosing the **N**o option in
   the `show hidden text` field of the **O**ptions
   command menu.

2. Switch to the outline mode by pressing **Shift-F2**.

3. Collapse all the body text and display all the headings you want to appear in the table of contents.

   If you want only the major section headings to appear, for instance, use the **Ctrl-Keypad+** command to specify Level 2 headings.

4. Use the **Library Table** command.

5. When the command menu appears, choose the **O**utline option in the `from` field.

Word compiles the table of contents and places it at the end of your document. Like the indexes Word compiles, the table of contents begins and ends with codes formatted as hidden text. Do not delete these codes. They will not print. Word needs them to locate the table in case you decide to compile the table of contents again.

To code headings so that Word will include them in the table of contents

1. Place the cursor at the beginning of the heading and press **Alt-E**.

2. Type .c..

3. Place the cursor on the space following the heading and press **Alt-E**.

4. Type ;.

   Your heading should conform to this coding scheme:

   ```
       .c.First Level of Heading;
      .c.:Second Level of Heading;
     .c.::Third Level of Heading;
    .c.:::Fourth Level of Heading;
   .c.::::Fifth Level of Heading;
   ```

5. After you finish coding all the entries, choose the **L**ibrary **T**able command, and choose the **C**odes option in the `from` field.

6. Carry out the command.

Tabs

You can change the default tab width (0.5 inches) for all paragraphs in a document (and all documents). You can also set custom tabs for each paragraph or paragraphs you select.

Version 5 improvements make setting custom tabs easy. As you use the Format Tab Set command, Word actively updates the screen to show the effects of the tab settings you choose. If you have a mouse and the ruler is visible, you can set, move, and cancel tabs without even using the Format Tab Set command. See RULER SETTINGS.

To change the default tab width

1. Choose the Options command.

2. Type a new measurement in the `default tab width` field.

3. Carry out the command.

To set a custom tab with the keyboard

1. Select the paragraph or paragraphs to which you would like the custom tabs to apply.

2. Choose the Format Tab Set command. Alternatively, use the Alt-F1 keyboard shortcut.

3. When the command menu appears, press F1 and use the arrow keys to move the highlight along the ruler.

   Use the right- and left-arrow keys to move the highlight one space at a time. If you press PgUp or PgDn, Word moves the highlight one inch at a time. Press End to go to the right indent mark, and Home to go to the left indent mark.

4. When the cursor is positioned where you want the tab stop, press Left, Right, Center, or Decimal to create a custom tab with the alignment you want.

   If you want to create a tab stop with a leader, type the leader character before the alignment letter. To create a right flush stop with a dot leader, for instance, type .R..

5. If you want to set another custom tab for the same paragraph, repeat steps 2 and 3.

6. Carry out the command.

After you carry out the command, Word places codes—Left, Right, Center, and Decimal—in the ruler showing the tab alignments you have set. If you chose a leader, Word also displays the leader character (a period, dash, or underscore) in front of the tab alignment code.

To set custom tabs with the mouse

1. Display the ruler by choosing the **Y**es option in the `show ruler` field of the **O**ptions menu. Alternatively, click the left button in the upper right corner of the display window.

2. Select the paragraph or paragraphs to which the tab stops will apply.

3. If you want an alignment other than left flush, click the L next to the left indent marker on the ruler until it displays the alignment code you want. Skip this step if you want left flush alignment.

4. To set the tab, click the ruler where you want the tab stop.

5. To set additional tabs, repeat steps 2 and 3.

To move a custom tab stop with the keyboard

1. Select the paragraph or paragraphs containing the tab you want to move.

2. Choose the **F**ormat **T**ab **S**et command or press **Alt-F1**.

3. Press **F1**. Then press the down- or up-arrow keys to select the tab you want to move.

Word highlights the tab code on the ruler.

4. Press **Ctrl-left arrow** to move the tab stop left, or press **Ctrl-right arrow** to move it right.

Word realigns the text right on the screen.

Note: If you "run over" another tab stop, Word will delete that tab stop.

5. To move other tabs, repeat steps 3 and 4.

6. Carry out the command.

To move a custom tab stop with the mouse

1. Point to the tab that you want to move on the ruler.

2. Hold down the right button and drag the tab stop to the new location.

To delete custom tabs with the keyboard

1. Select the paragraph or paragraphs that contain the custom tab. Then choose Format Tab Set or press Alt-F1.

2. Press the down-arrow key to select the tab you want to delete.

3. Press Del to remove the tab.

   Alternatively, press Ctrl-Del to remove the tab and all the custom tabs to the right.

4. To delete additional tabs, repeat steps 2 and 3.

5. Carry out the command.

To delete custom tabs with the mouse

1. Point to the tab on the ruler.

2. Click both buttons.

3. To delete additional tabs, repeat steps 1 and 2.

To delete all custom tab stops

Choose the Format Tabs Reset-all command to cancel all custom tab stops for the selected paragraph or paragraphs.

Special Keys
When Using Format Tab Set

Key	Effect
F1	Select tab stops on ruler
Down arrow	Select next tab stop right (after pressing F1)

Up arrow	Select next tab stop left (after pressing F1)
Right arrow	Move highlight right on ruler
Left arrow	Move highlight left on ruler
PgUp	Move highlight one inch left on ruler
PgDn	Move highlight one inch right on ruler
Ins	Create custom tab stop and clear menu for setting additional ones
Del	Delete custom tab stop
Ctrl-Del	Delete custom tab stop and all custom tab stops to right of cursor

Text Mode

Word takes full advantage of your video adapter's capabilities. With most adapters, you can choose between GRAPHICS MODE and the text mode. Because text mode is the faster of the two, most Word users prefer to scroll and edit in this mode. In text mode, however, you will not see character emphases other than boldface and underlining, and you cannot use Print preView (see PREVIEWING YOUR DOCUMENT). Switch to graphics mode when you need to see all your formatting. If you are in text mode when you choose Print preView, Word switches to graphics mode automatically.

To choose the display mode

1. Use the Options command and highlight the `display mode` field.

2. Press F1 to view the list of available modes. Select the text mode, and press Enter.

To toggle between the last two modes you have chosen, press Alt-F9.

Thesaurus

Use thEsaurus to view a list of synonyms for the word
you select. If you prefer one of the synonyms, you can
insert it into your document with a keystroke.

To look up a word in the Thesaurus

1. Press F8 or click the right mouse button to highlight
   the word you want to look up.

2. Choose the Library thEsaurus command.
   Alternatively, use the Ctrl-F6 keyboard shortcut.

   If Thesaurus does not list the word you have chosen,
   it checks to see whether the word is listed in another
   form. For instance, if you highlight "officiously"
   and use Thesaurus, you will see synonyms for
   "officious."

   If Thesaurus cannot find the word or any of its roots,
   you will see the message, The word was not
   found. Choose another word to look
   up. You will see a list of 30 words closest in
   spelling to the word you highlighted. Use the arrow
   keys to highlight another word on the list, or press
   Esc.

3. When the Thesaurus window appears, use the arrow
   keys to highlight the word you want from the list.

4. Press Enter to insert the word you have highlighted
   into your document (mouse users: point to the
   synonym you want and click the right button). Word
   makes the substitution automatically. Alternatively,
   press Esc to leave Thesaurus without making a
   change.

To see synonyms of words in a Thesaurus list

1. Open the Thesaurus by highlighting a word and
   pressing Ctrl-F6.

2. Highlight a word in the synonym list.

3. Press Ctrl-F6 again (mouse users: click the words
   CTRL-F6:look up on the Thesaurus window's
   bottom border).

4. When the new synonym list appears, choose a synonym. Press **Enter** (or click the right button) to insert the word in your document. Alternatively, press **Ctrl-F6** to see more synonyms.

You can continue viewing synonyms of synonyms indefinitely. To see the previous list of synonyms, press **Ctrl-PgUp** or click the words `Ctrl-PgUp:last word` on the bottom window border.

Transposing Text

Mouse users can quickly transpose characters, words, and sentences with the following techniques.

To transpose characters, words, or sentences

1. Select the second unit of text you want to transpose, using the text selection techniques introduced in this chapter.

   To transpose characters, select the second character. To transpose words, select the second word, and to transpose sentences, select the second sentence.

2. Point to the first unit of text (character, word, or sentence), and press the **Ctrl** key.

3. To transpose characters, click the left button. To transpose words, click the right button. To transpose sentences, click both buttons.

Tutorial Help

When you use **H**elp, you can choose Quick Help, which displays help screens on a subject (see HELP). If you need more guidance, you can choose Tutorial Help, which displays lessons from LEARNING WORD.

To get Tutorial Help on a command or command field

1. Highlight the command or field you do not understand.

2. Press **Alt-H** to display the **H**elp command menu and the Quick Help screen for the command or field.

3. Choose the **T**utorial option from the **H**elp command menu.

4. Choose the **L**esson option on the **T**utorial command submenu.

To choose a tutorial from an index of topics covered

1. Choose the **H**elp command or click the Help mark.

2. When the **H**elp command menu appears, choose the **T**utorial option.

3. When the **T**utorial submenu appears, choose the **I**ndex option.

4. Use the arrow keys or the mouse to highlight the lesson you want, and press **Enter**.

To quit Tutorial Help at any time

Press **Ctrl-Q** to quit Tutorial Help. To quit the **H**elp command menu, choose **E**xit.

Undo

You can reverse the effects of editing and formatting actions, and many commands, by choosing **U**ndo. However, you must use the command immediately after performing the action or using the command. If you want to restore your action or command, press **U**ndo again.

To cancel your last editing action

Choose the **U**ndo command or press **Shift-F1** immediately after inserting, deleting, moving, or copying text.

Effects of Undo on Editing Actions

Last editing operation	Effect of Pressing Undo
Text copied to Scrap	Previous Scrap contents restored.
Text inserted from Scrap	Insertion canceled.
Text copied with mouse	Copied text disappears.
Text moved with mouse	Move canceled, text reappears in original position with highlighting.
Text deleted to Scrap	Deletion canceled; text reappears in original position with highlighting.
Text deleted with Bksp	Deletion canceled; text restored.

To cancel your last formatting action

Choose the Undo command or press **Shift-F1** immediately after using the Format command or the SPEED KEY SHORTCUTS.

To cancel your last command

Choose the Undo command or press **Shift-F1** immediately after using any of the following commands: Copy, Delete, Format, Format repLace, Insert, Library Autosort, Library Hyphenate, Library Link, Library Number, Library Spell, Library Table, Library thEsaurus, Replace, Transfer Merge, or Undo.

Effects of Undo after Using Commands

Last command used	Effect of Pressing Undo
Copy	Previous contents of Scrap restored.
Format	Formatting canceled.
Format repLace	Operation canceled and all substitutions restored to original format.

Gallery	No effect. Use Exit to return to your document.
Help	No effect. Use Exit to return to your document.
Insert	Insertion canceled.
Jump	No effect.
Library Autosort	Sort canceled; text returns to order before command was given.
Library Hyphenate	Hyphenation canceled; all hyphens inserted by command are removed.
Library Index	Index just created is removed.
Library Number	Numbering canceled and numbers removed.
Library Run	No effect; give a DOS command and press a key to return to Word.
Library Spell	Cancels all changes made in Spell session.
Library Table	Table just created is removed.
Library thEsaurus	Cancels word substitution and restores original.
Options	No effect. To cancel choices in the Options menu, use the command again and restore the original settings.
Print	No effect. Press Esc to stop printing.
Quit	No effect. If you see a message, press Esc to return to Word.
RepLace	Word substitutions removed and originals restored throughout document.
Search	No effect. Press Esc to cancel search while still in progress.

Transfer Load	No effect.
Transfer Merge	No effect.
Undo	Undoes effect of last Undo command; restores changes.

Upper- and Lowercase

New to Word 5 is a command, Ctrl-F4, that controls uppercase and lowercase formatting. You can still format characters in uppercase by choosing the Yes option in the uppercase field of the Format Character command. This format will be lost if you save your document in any format other than Word's.

You will probably save your document without formatting, for instance, so that you can upload it via electronic mail links or swap it with colleagues who use other word processing programs. That is not true in the case formatting done with Ctrl-F4. When you choose case (upper or lower) with Ctrl-F4, the text remains as it appears on the screen, even if you save your file without formatting.

To use Ctrl-F4 to change case formatting

1. Select the text you want to change.

2. Press Ctrl-F4 once, and the text appears in lowercase letters.

If you press Ctrl-F4 again, the text appears in all uppercase letters. If you press Ctrl-F4 a third time, the text appears with the first letter of each word capitalized.

Windows

Word can display up to eight windows on the screen simultaneously. You can view different parts of the same document, or you can view different documents, up to the maximum of eight. At a keystroke, you can "zoom" a window to full size, and "unzoom" it again, revealing the other windows behind it.

To open a window with the keyboard

1. Choose the **W**indow **S**plit command.

2. Choose the **H**orizontal or **V**ertical options.

3. When the **W**indow **S**plit **H**orizontal or **W**indow **S**plit **V**ertical command menu appears, press **F1** in the `at line` field to activate a special cursor on the left window border. Use the arrow keys to move the cursor to the place you want the window split.

   Alternatively, just type a number in the `at line` field.

4. To clear the new window so that it displays a new, blank document, choose the **Y**es option in the `clear new window` field.

   By default, this option is set to **N**o, so if you split the screen without changing this option, Word will display an additional window on the document that is already open.

5. Carry out the command.

To open a window with the mouse

1. To split the screen vertically, point to the place on the top border where you want the split to occur. To split the screen horizontally, point to the right border.

2. When the mouse pointer changes shape (a big rectangle in text mode or a square outline in graphics mode), click the left button to split the screen without clearing the new window. To clear the new window, click the right button instead.

Note: If you have displayed the ruler, hold down the **Alt** key before clicking the top border.

When more than one window is open, only one is active. The active window contains the cursor, and its number is highlighted.

To make another window active with the keyboard

Press **F1** to make the next window active. If Window 1 is active, pressing **F1** activates Window 2, and so on. Keep pressing **F1** to reactivate Window 1.

To make another window active with the mouse

1. Point to text in the window you want to activate. Alternatively, point to the window number.

   If you activate the window by clicking the window number, you preserve the selection in the window.

2. Click the left or right button.

To size a window with the keyboard

1. Activate the window you want to move.

2. Choose the **Window Move** command.

3. When the **Window Move** command menu appears, select the `to row` field and press **F1**. Move the special cursor to the row where you want the window's lower right corner.

   Alternatively, type a row number in this field.

4. Now select the `column` field and press **F1**. Move the special cursor to the column where you want the window's lower right corner. Alternatively, type a column number in this field.

Note: You cannot change the lower right corner of the lower right window. To change its size, size one of the windows above it or below it. Also remember that you cannot shrink a window if there is no other window to take its place.

To size windows with the mouse

1. Move the pointer to window's lower right corner.

2. When the mouse pointer changes shape (a large rectangle in text mode or an arrow pointing four ways in graphics mode), click either button and drag the mouse to stretch the window to the desired size.

3. Release the mouse button.

To zoom a window with the keyboard

1. Make the window active.

2. Press **Ctrl-F1** to toggle the zoom mode on.

The code ZM appears in the key status indicator on the status line.

To move to the next window in the sequence while in zoom mode, just press **F1**.

To unzoom a window, just press **Ctrl-F1** again.

To zoom a window with the mouse

1. Point to the window number.

2. Click the right mouse button.

To move to the next window in the zoom mode with the mouse

1. Point to the window number of the window that is displayed.

2. Click the left mouse button.

The next window in the sequence is displayed, zoomed to full size.

To unzoom a window with the mouse

1. Point to the window number of a zoomed window.

2. Click the right mouse button.

To close windows with the keyboard

1. Make active the window you want to close. If you want to save the text in it, use the **T**ransfer **S**ave command.

2. Choose the **W**indow **C**lose command. Make sure that the correct window number is displayed.

3. Carry out the command.

To close windows with the mouse

1. Position the pointer on the top or right window border.

2. When the pointer shape changes, click both mouse buttons.

If you see the message, Enter Y to save changes to document, N to lose

`changes, or Esc to cancel,` you have not
saved the window's text. Press **Y** to save or **N** to
abandon.

To copy or move text between two parts of the same document using windows

1. Split the screen horizontally so that the new window is not cleared.

   Two windows are open on the same document.

2. Scroll the bottom screen to the place where you want the text copied or moved.

3. Make the top window active, and select the text to be copied or moved. Use the **C**opy command (or **Alt-F3**) to copy the text to the Scrap. Alternatively, use the **D**elete command (or the **Del** key) to delete the text to the scrap.

4. Make the bottom window active, and position the cursor where you want the text stored in the Scrap to appear. Then choose the **I**nsert command (or press **Ins**).

To copy or move text between two documents using windows

1. Split the screen horizontally and clear the new window.

   The top screen shows your document, but the bottom screen is blank.

2. Use the **T**ransfer **L**oad command to load the second document into the bottom window.

3. Activate the window in which you want to insert the text to be copied or moved.

4. Now activate the other window, and select the text to be copied or moved. Use the **C**opy command (or **Alt-F3**) to copy the text to the Scrap. Alternatively, use the **D**elete command (or the **Del** key) to delete the text to the scrap.

5. Make the other window active, and position the cursor where you want the text stored in the Scrap to appear. Then choose the **I**nsert command (or press **Ins**).

Index

A

Add command, 120
annotations, 45
    jump to, 70
arithmetic operators, 83
ASCII files, 8
AUTOEXEC.BAT file, 31, 76
automatic styles, 8-11

B

backup copies of files, 12-13
boilerplate documents, 14
    see also form letters
    linking, 37
bold text, 17
bookmarks, 14-16
    canceling, 15-16
    cross-reference of page
        number, 26-27
    jump to, 70
borders, 16-17
boxes, 16-17

C

CAPTURE.COM utility, 54
CD (DOS) command, 123
centimeters, 84
characters
    formatting, 17-18
    speed key shortcuts, 116
    positioning, 18-19
    superscript or subscript, 18-19
colors, customizing screen, 22
Column-select mode, 84
columns, 22-23
    column indicator in command
        area, 23
    selecting, 110-111
    snaking, 114-115
command area, 23-24
    key status indicator, 24
    line number indicator, 23
    page and column indicators,
        23
    save indicator, 24
    Scrap, 24
Command mode, 19-20
commands
    commands listed by name
    canceling, 17
    choosing, 19-21
Copy command, 25-26, 39, 51-
    52, 79, 143
copying
    formats, 24-25
    text, 25-26
Correct command, 117, 119

cross-references in text, 26-27
cursor movement, 27-28

D

data document, 80
    form letters, 46-47
dates
    formatting, 30
    inserting in documents, 30-31
default
    directory, 31-32
    formats, 32-33
    style sheet (NORMAL.STY),
        32
Delete command, 34, 39, 51-52,
    85, 143
dictionaries, 119-121
directories
    default, 31-32
    searching other for
        documents, 38
division
    breaks, 34-35
    mark, 36
documents
    attach different style sheet,
        126
    boilerplate, 14, 37
    change default character font,
        10-11
    chapters, 34-35
    cross-references, 26-27
    customizing document list, 39
    data, 80
    dictionaries, 120
    division breaks, 34-35
    forms, 49-50
    headers and footers, 56-58
    linking, 37
    loading, 75-77
    outline from, 90-91
    previewing, 96-98
    printing, 99-101
    restructure by rearranging
        outline, 90
    retrieving, 38-39
    return from help, 60
    searching for, 38-39
    starting new, 21
    spreadsheets linking to, 122-
        123
DOS, accessing, 2-3

E

Edit command, 39-40
Elite, 85
endnotes, 42-45
Exit command, 60

F

file extensions
  .CMP, 121
  .DOC, 12
  .MAC, 78
  .PRD, 99
files
  ASCII, 8
  AUTOEXEC.BAT, 31, 76
  automatically saving changes,
    11
  backup copies, 12-13
  deleting, 3
  INDEX.MAC, 65-66
  MACRO.GLY, 65
  marking, 12
  NORMAL.GLY, 53
  NORMAL.STY, 9-11, 59,
    125-126
  removing temporary, 21
  saving, 2, 11, 106-107
  SPECIALS.CMP, 120
  SPELL-AM.CMP, 120
  SPELL-AM.LEX, 120
  UPDAT-AM.CMP, 120
floppy drive system, starting
  Microsoft Word, 123-124
fonts, 40-42
footers, 56-58
footnotes, 42-45
  change default, 9-10
  inserting, 43
  jump to, 70
  moving, 44
  window, 7, 44-45
form letters, 45-49
  see also boilerplate
Format Annotation command, 6
Format Bookmark command, 15,
  26
Format Border command, 16,
  55-58
Format Character command, 10,
  17, 41-42, 93
Format command, 9, 40
Format Division command, 92
Format Division Layout
  command, 22, 35, 42, 81,
  114-115
Format Division Line-Numbers
  command, 73-74
Format Division Margins
  command, 33, 80-82, 94
Format Division Page-Numbers
  command, 8, 92-93, 96
Format Footnote command, 8, 43
Format Paragraph command, 3-
  4, 10, 13-14, 56, 58, 63,
  75, 91
Format Position command, 4-5,
  55
Format Replace Character
  command, 104

Format Replace Paragraph
  command, 104
Format Revision-Marks Accept-
  Revisions command, 103
Format Revision-Marks Options
  command, 102
Format Revision-Marks Search
  command, 103
Format Revision-Marks Undo-
  Revisions command, 103
Format Running-Head
  command, 57-58, 93, 96
Format Search Character
  command, 108-109
Format Search Paragraph
  command, 109
Format Stylesheet Attach
  command, 126
Format Stylesheet Record
  command, 59, 125-126
Format Tab Set command, 130-
  132
Format Tabs Reset-All
  command, 132
formats
  copying, 24-25
  default, 32-33
  options, 84-85
  replacing, 103-104
  searching for, 108-109
forms, 49-50
frames, 4-6
function keys, 50-51
  see also keys
  with Alt, 51
  with Ctrl, 51
  with Shift, 50

G

Gallery command, 9-10, 40
glossaries, 51-53
  dateprint, 31
  entries, 51-53
  moving text, 85-86
  timeprint, 31
graphics, 54-55
  adding captions, 55
  anchoring, 4-6
  borders and shading, 54-55
  importing, 54
  shading, 54-55
graphics mode, 55-56

H

hanging indentation, 56
hard disk system, starting
  Microsoft Word, 123
headers, 56-58
  see also pages and running
  heads
headings, 58-59
  outlines, 59

help, 59-60
    tutorial, 135-136
Help command, 40, 60, 136
hidden text, 60-61
Hidden Text command (.G.), 54
hyphens, 61-62

I

inches, 84 indenting text, 62-64
    first line indent symbol (⌐), 64
    left indent symbol ([), 64
INDEX.MAC file, 65-66
indexing, 64-68
Insert command, 7, 9-10, 25-26,
    30-31, 40, 52, 65, 68, 78-
    79, 93, 143-144
Insert mode, 3

J

Jump Annotation command, 7,
    70
Jump Bookmark command, 15-
    16, 70
Jump command, 40
Jump Footnote command, 43-44,
    70
Jump Page command, 69
justifying text, 71

K

key status indicator
    codes, 71
    in command area, 24
keyboard
    choosing commands, 19-20
    collapse subheadings, 89
    copying
        paragraph
            format, 25
            text, 26
    expand subheadings, 90
    open window, 140
    selecting text, 111
    set custom tab, 130-131
    size window, 141
    zoom window, 141-142
keys
    Alt-0 (subheading down a
        level), 88-90
    Alt-2 (double-space text), 75
    Alt-9 (paragraph as outline
        heading), 88, 90
    Alt-B (bold text), 17
    Alt-C (centered text), 3-4, 55,
        87, 93
    Alt-E (hidden text), 49, 60-
        61, 66
    Alt-equal (superscript), 18-19
    Alt-F1 (tab set), 130-132
    Alt-F2 (footer), 57
    Alt-F3 (copy), 26, 143
    Alt-F4 (show), 113-114

Alt-F5 (jump to page), 69
Alt-F6 (spell), 117-118
Alt-F7 (line break display on/
    off), 30, 72
Alt-F8 (select font), 41
Alt-F9 (toggle between
    modes), 56, 133
Alt-F10 (record style), 59,
    125-126
Alt-H (help), 60, 136
Alt-hyphen (subscript), 18-19
Alt-J (justify text), 3-4, 71
Alt-M (increase left
    indent), 63
Alt-N (left indent), 63
Alt-O (insert blank line), 13-
    14, 96
Alt-P (format), 4, 13, 63, 75,
    95
Alt-P (flush left), 57
Alt-plus (superscript), 43
Alt-Q (indent left and
    right), 63
Alt-R (flush right), 3-4, 57, 93
Alt-space bar (turn feature
    off), 17-18, 41
Alt-U (underscored text), 17
Arrow (select character), 111
Backspace (delete
    character), 34
Ctrl-< (back one field), 50
Ctrl-> (next field), 50
Ctrl-Enter (division break),
    35, 81, 115
Ctrl-F1 (toggle zoom), 141-
    142
Ctrl-F2 (header), 57
Ctrl-F3 (Step mode), 79
Ctrl-F4 (toggle case), 139
Ctrl-F5 (line draw), 73
Ctrl-F6 (Thesaurus), 134-135
Ctrl-F7 (load), 76
Ctrl-F8 (print), 99
Ctrl-F9 (print preview), 97
Ctrl-F10 (save), 106
Ctrl-hyphen (optional
    hyphen), 62
Ctrl-PgUp (beginning of
    document), 93
Ctrl-Shift-Enter (page break),
    92
Ctrl-Shift-hyphen
    (nonbreaking hyphen), 62
Ctrl-space bar (mark all files),
    12, 61
Ctrl-[(left chevron [<<]), 47,
    79-80
Ctrl-] (right chevron [>>]), 47,
    49, 79-80
cursor-movement, 28
Del (delete character to
    Scrap), 7, 34-35
End (select character), 111
Esc, 79

F1 (list files), 36, 41, 52, 55, 77, 122
F2 (Calculate), 83-84
F3 (glossary), 31, 52, 86-87
F4 (repeat), 25-26
F5 (insert/overtype mode), 3, 91
F6 (Extend-selection), 112
F7 (select previous word), 111
F8 (select next word), 111
F9 (select previous paragraph), 111
F10 (select next paragraph), 111
Home (select character), 111
hyphen (-), 62
Ins, 7, 26, 68
Scroll Lock, 27-28
Shift, 112
Shift-Ctrl-space bar (unmark all files), 12
Shift-Del (delete character), 34
Shift-F1 (undo), 136-139
Shift-F2 (Outline mode), 88, 90, 128
Shift-F3 (record macro), 78
Shift-F4 (search), 110
Shift-F5 (Outline organize mode), 90
Shift-F6 (column select), 84, 111
Shift-F7 (select previous sentence), 111
Shift-F8 (select next sentence), 111
Shift-F9 (select current line), 111
Shift-F10 (select entire document), 4, 14, 42, 63-64, 71, 75, 103, 111, 122
Shift-Ins (replace selection with Scrap), 34
Shift-Tab (move left and up), 19-20
Tab (move right and down), 19-20

L

labels, mailing, 80-82
Library Autosort command, 115
Library command, 40
Library Document-retrieval command, 12-13, 38-39, 101, 128
Library Index command, 68
Library Link Document command, 14, 37
Library Link Graphic command, 4-5, 54
Library Link Spreadsheet command, 122
Library Number command, 91
Library Run command, 2, 6, 36

Library Spell command, 117-119
Library Table command, 129
Library Thesaurus command, 134
Line Draw mode, 72-73
line number
    indicator, 23
    in text, 73-74
lines, 85
    breaks, 29
    spacing in paragraphs, 75
linking documents, 37

M

MACRO.GLY file, 65
macros, 77-79
mailing labels, 80-82
margins, 82-83
math, 83-84
measurement codes, 84-85
menus
    Command, 29
    Document-retrieval, 38
    Edit command, 39-40
    Format Character, 18, 41, 60-61
    Library Run, 2
    Options, 38, 51, 60-61, 69, 79, 124
    Print Options, 99-100
    Spell, 118, 120
Microsoft Word
    clearing, 21
    quitting, 101-102
    tutorial, 72
modes
    Column-select, 84
    Command, 19-20
    Graphics, 55-56
    Insert, 3
    Line Draw, 72-73
    Outline, 87-91
    Overtype, 3, 91
    Record-macro, 78
    Scroll Lock, 27
    Show Layout, 113
    Step, 79
    Text, 133
mouse
    choosing commands, 20-21
    collapse subheadings, 89
    copying, 24-26
    expand subheadings, 89
    indenting text, 64
    jump to page, 70
    open window, 140
    scrolling, 107-108
    selecting text, 112-113
    set custom tabs, 131
    size window, 141
    zoom window, 142

N

Newline command, 86
NORMAL.STY file, 9-11, 32,
   125-126

O

Options command, 11, 22, 25,
   29-30, 33, 40, 55, 61, 74,
   84, 87, 120
Outline mode, 87-91
outlines, 88-91
overtype mode, 3, 91

P

page breaks, 91-92
   control at division break, 35
   previewing, 98
page indicator in command area,
   23
page number
   change default character
     format, 9
   cross-reference of bookmark,
     26-27
pages
   formats, 92
   jumping to, 69-70
   numbering, 92-93
   preventing bad page breaks,
     58
   running heads, 57-58
   size of, 94
pagination, 94
paragraph marks, 95-96
   display, 29
   start new line without, 86
paragraphs
   anchoring, 4-6
   blank lines, 13-14, 95
   borders, 16
   boxes, 16
   change alignment, 3-4
   formats, 4, 94-95
     side-by-side, 23
     speed key shortcuts, 116-
       117
   hanging indentation, 56
   indentation, 62-64, 95
   joining, 68-69
   line spacing, 75
   remove borders or boxes, 16-
     17
   side-by-side, 113-114
   splitting, 121
Pica, 84
points, 85
previewing
   documents, 96-98
   page breaks, 98
Print command, 40
Print Merge command, 45

Print Merge Printer command,
   48, 80, 82
Print Options command, 55, 61,
   99-100
Print Preview command, 54, 96
Print Printer command, 31, 50,
   99-100
Print Queued Continue
   command, 101
Print Queued Pause command,
   101
Print Queued Restart command,
   101
Print Queued Stop command,
   101
Print Repaginate command, 98
printers, selecting, 99
printing
   documents, 99-101
   form letters, 48-49
   line numbers, 73
   time or date, 31
Proof command, 118

Q

Query command, 12, 38
Quick Help *see* help
Quit command, 40, 101
quitting Word, 101-102

R

Record-macro mode, 78
redlining text, 102-103
Replace command, 40, 104-105
replacing
   formats, 103-104
   text, 104-105
retrieving documents, 38-39
ruler settings, 105-106
running heads, add page numbers
   to, 93

S

SAVE indicator in command
   area, 24
saving files, 106-107
Scrap, 25, 33, 107
   in command area, 24
   moving text with, 85
screen
   customizing, 22, 29-30
   Quick Help, 136
Scroll Lock mode, 27
scrolling
   with mouse, 107-108
   screen, 27-28
Search command, 40, 109-110
searching
   formats, 108-109
   text, 109-110
series code name, 87
series items, numbering, 87

Show Layout mode, 113
sorting text, 115
SPECIALS.CMP file, 120
speed key shortcuts
    see also keys
    character formatting, 116
    create new, 126
    modify existing, 125
    paragraph formatting, 116-117
Spell command, 121
Spell Options command, 121
SPELL-AM.CMP file, 120
SPELL-AM.LEX file, 120
spell-checking text, 117-121
spreadsheets, linking to
    documents, 122-123
start-up options, 124
Step mode, 79
style sheets, 124-126
styles, automatic, 8-11
subheadings, 88-90
subscript, 18-19
summary sheets, 127-128
superscript, 18-19
synonyms, 134-135

T

table of contents, 128-129
tables, numbering automatically,
    87
tabs, 130-133
text
    adding, 3
    aligning, 3-4, 94
    anchoring, 4-6
    annotating, 6-7
    blank lines in, 13-14
    bold, 17
    copying, 25-26
    deleting, 33-34
    double-spacing, 75
    formatting, 17
    hidden, 60-61
    importing from another Word
        document, 37
    indenting, 62-64
    inserting, 68
    justifying, 71
    line breaks, 72
    line numbers, 73-74
    line spacing, 95
    marking as bookmarks, 15
    moving, 85-86
    naming ranges of
        (bookmarks), 14
    paginating, 94
    redlining, 102-103
    repeating, 26
    replacing, 104-105
    revising in notes, 43-44
    searching for, 109-110
    selecting, 111-113
    sorting, 115

spell-checking, 117-121
temporary storage, 107
transposing, 135
underscored, 17
upper- and lowercase, 139
Text mode, 133
thesaurus, 134-135
time
    formatting, 30
    inserting in documents, 30-31
Transfer Allsave command, 2,
    107
Transfer Clear All command, 21
Transfer Clear Window
    command, 21, 50
Transfer command, 40
Transfer Delete command, 3, 36
Transfer Glossary Clear
    command, 52, 86
Transfer Glossary Load
    command, 53, 65
Transfer Glossary Save
    command, 53, 86
Transfer Load command, 31, 76-
    77, 143
Transfer Options command, 31
Transfer Save All command, 24
Transfer Save command, 2, 8-11,
    31, 48, 50, 106, 127
Tutorial Help, 135-136
    see also help

U

Undo command, 17, 40, 118-
    119, 136-139
UPDAT-AM.CMP file, 120
uppercase text, 139
utility, CAPTURE.COM, 54

W

Window Close command, 45,
    142
Window command, 40
Window Move command, 141
Window Split command, 140
Window Split Footnote
    command, 44
windows, 139-144
    clearing, 21
    closing, 142-143
    copying text, 143-144
    footnote, 44-45
    hide borders, 29
    open, 140
    size, 141
    zoom, 141-142
words, hyphenating, 61-62